The CHURCH AT Washington, New Hampshire

The

CHURCH AT

Washington, New Hampshire

The author assumes full responsibility for the accuracy of all facts and quotations as cited in this book.

Texts credited to NIV are from the *Holy Bible, New International Version.* Copyright © 1973, 1978, 1984, International Bible Society. Used by permission of Zondervan Bible Publishers.

This book was
Copyedited by James Cavil
Interior design by Mark Ford
Cover design by Square One Design
Cover photo by Edward Runnals
Typeset: Bembo 12/15

PRINTED IN U.S.A.

06   05   04   03   02   5   4   3   2   1

R&H Cataloging Service
Ford, Mark
    The church at Washington, New Hampshire: Cradle of Seventh-day Adventism.

    1. Washington, New Hampshire, Seventh-day Adventist Church.   I. Title.

286.73209742

ISBN 0-8280-1683-6

To Cynthia

Charles Fitch, assisted by Apollos Hale, designed the famous 1843 prophetic chart that was adopted by the Millerite Adventist general conference in Boston, Massachusetts, May 1842. The chart was printed on cloth, and its large figures and images were designed to make the time prophecies easier to present to the public. In *Early Writings* Ellen White wrote that she was shown in vision that, in spite of its mistake in calculating the end of the 2300 days, "the 1843 chart was directed by the hand of the Lord" (p. 74). *Photo and text provided by the Ellen G. White Estate.*

ACKNOWLEDGMENTS

This book was derived from the documentary video of the same name, conceived by the Ellen G. White Estate, and produced by the Review and Herald Publishing Association. Special thanks goes to Juan Carlos Viera, former director of the White Estate, who initiated the project; to James Nix, the current director, and Tim Poirier, senior archivist, for their patience and untiring attention to the many details such a project entails; to Pat Fritz, editor of New Media Publications at the Review, where this project was developed; and to Jeannette Johnson, acquisitions editor at the Review, who saw light in the idea of a companion book and made it happen; to Tompaul Wheeler, budding videographer and peerless reporter, for the dozens of tightly-worded photo captions he prepared; to Gwen Gaskell at the Washington, New Hampshire, Historical Society for opening the doors of the archives to us; to Mark Harris, the current pastor of the Washington, New Hampshire, church, and Phil Barker, brother to Gwen, who together cut a hole in two feet of ice on Millen Pond in driving sleet for just four seconds of fame; and to Ron Jager, the retired teacher of philosophy at Yale University, who by turns was our expert historian, indispensable guide, golden-voiced narrator, and respected friend in the course of this work.

And to Elizabeth Howe, who tirelessly searched through stacks of documents, papers, books, and archives from across the country to find just the right picture, to verify the exact quotation, and to uncover the first original source. Her enthusiasm, energy, and encouragement were invaluable. For all she accomplished, I am immensely grateful.

The Washington story was greatly influenced by the teachings of William Miller, a farmer, justice of the peace, sheriff, and Baptist preacher who, from 1831 to 1844, preached the imminent return of Christ. His work set the stage for what later became the Seventh-day Adventist Church. *Portrait provided by the Ellen G. White Estate.*

THE ADVENT HERALD,

AND SIGNS OF THE TIMES REPORTER.

BEHOLD! THE BRIDEGROOM COMETH!! GO YE OUT TO MEET HIM!!!

VOL. VIII. NO. 11.　　　Boston, Wednesday, October 16, 1844.　　　WHOLE NO. 181.

THE ADVENT HERALD

☞ As the date of the present number of the Herald is our last day of publication before the tenth day of the seventh month, we shall make no provision for issuing a paper for the week following. And as we are shut up to this faith,—by the sounding of this cry at midnight, during the tarrying of the vision, when we had all slumbered and slept, and at the very point when all the periods, according to our chronology and date of their commencement, terminate—we feel called upon to suspend our labors and await the result. Behold, the Bridegroom cometh; go ye out to meet him! is the cry that is being sounded in our ears; and may we all, with our lamps trimmed and burning, be prepared for His glorious appearing.　　J. V. HIMES.

Oct. 8.

"Go ye out to meet Him."

THE TENTH DAY OF THE SEVENTH MONTH.

I take up my pen with feelings such as I never before experienced. Beyond a doubt, in my mind, the *tenth day of the seventh month* will usher in the coming of our Lord Jesus Christ in the clouds of heaven. We are then within a *few days* of that event. Awful moment to those who are unprepared —but glorious to those who are ready. I feel that I am making the *last appeal* that I shall ever make through the press. My heart is full. I see the ungodly and the sinner disappearing from my view, and there now stands before my mind the *professed believers* in the Lord's near approach. But what shall I say to them? Alas! we have all been *slumbering and sleeping*—both the *wise* and the *foolish*; but so our Savior told us it would be; and "thus the Scriptures are fulfilled," and it is the last prophecy relating to the events to precede the *personal advent* of our Lord; now comes the *True Midnight Cry*. The previous, was but the *alarm*. Now the *real one is sounding*; and Oh, how solemn the hour. The "virgins" have been *asleep* or *slumbering*; yes, all of us. Asleep *on the time*: that is the point. Some have indeed preached the *seventh month*, but it has with *doubt* whether it is *this year* or some other: and that doubt is now removed from my mind. "Behold, the Bridegroom cometh," This Year, "Go ye out to meet him." We have done with the nominal churches and all the wicked, except so far as *this* very may affect them: our work is now to wake up the "virgins" who "took their lamps and went forth to meet the Bridegroom." Where are we now? "If the vision *tarry*, wait for it." Is not that our answer since last March and April? Yes. What happened while the bridegroom *tarried*!— The virgins all slumbered and slept, did they not! Christ's word's not failed; and "the Scriptures cannot be broken," and it is of no use for us to pretend that we have been awake: we have been slumbering; not on the *fact* of Christ's coming, but on the *time*. We came into the *tarrying time*—we did not know "*how long*" it would tarry, and on that point we have slumbered—some of us have said, in our sleep, "Don't fix *another* time," so we slept. Now the trouble is to wake us up, Lord help, for vain is the help of man. Wake *thyself*, Lord. O, that the "*Father*" may now "make known" the *time*.

Peter, 1st Epistle, chap. i. 11, positively declares that the Spirit of Christ, in the prophets, did *testify the time* for the sufferings of Christ and the glory that should follow, and gives us to understand, in the 13th verse, that that glory was to be "at the *revelation* of Jesus Christ." Speaking of the prophets, Peter says—"Searching what, or what manner of time the Spirit of Christ, which was in them did signify, when it testified beforehand the sufferings of Christ, and the glory that should follow. Wherefore gird up the loins of your mind, be sober, and hope to the end for the grace that is to be brought unto you at the revelation of Jesus Christ." Here we have the fact stated that the Spirit of Christ did reveal to the prophets the *time* not only of Christ's sufferings, but of his glory, or "revelation." Peter tells us the time revealed was not literal but *symbolical*. "What *manner* of *time*!" He also says that "the angels desire to look into" these "things." By turning to the 12th chapter of Daniel, we find, that after the angel had finished the detailed explanation of the visions, and wound up with the standing up of Michael, [*one like God*—the Son of God,] the resurrection of the saints, and those that had turned many to righteousness shine as the stars, &c., that Daniel sees, verse 5, two angels, "and one said to the man clothed in linen, which was upon the waters of the river — *how long* shall it be to *the end* of these wonders?" Here is an inquiry about *time*, by the angels. Well, Peter said the angels desired to look into." Did they get an answer! See Dan. xii. 7—"And I heard the man clothed in linen, which was upon the waters of the river, when he held up his right hand and his left hand unto heaven, and sware by Him that liveth forever, it shall be for a *time*, times an half; and when he shall have accomplished to scatter the power of the holy people, all these things shall be finished." This person thus swearing, was none other than the Lord Jesus Christ; and he *sware to time*. Yea, to time connected with the second advent, the resurrection, and the glorification of his people. The time, however, is symbolical. But will any man dare take the blasphemous position that the Lord Jesus sware to time that meant nothing; or, which is the same thing, sware, with the most solemn oath, to time that he intended should *never be understood?* Such a position, one would suppose, is blasphemous enough to make a devil tremble; for, it is virtually charging the Lord of Glory with *swearing a lie!* Beware, O vain man, how you thus charge the Son of God. Time is revealed. But it cannot be understood without obeying Christ, and "inquiring and *searching diligently* what, and *what manner* of time." Those who are too indolent to search, or who are afraid to follow truth when they find it, for fear of man, whose breath is in his nostrils, will of course remain in ignorance of time, and that day, most likely, will come upon them unawares.

I will now present a brief argument from the types to show that the *tenth day* of the *seventh month* is the time in the year to look for our *coming* Lord. Matt. v. 17, 18—Our Lord says, "Think not that I am come to destroy the law or the prophets; I am not come to destroy, but to fulfil. For verily I say unto you, Till heaven and earth pass, one *jot or one tittle* shall in no wise pass from the law, till all be fulfilled." This must relate to the law of types as well as the moral law. Let us now inquire how the types have been fulfilled. The first we will notice is the slaying of the paschal lamb, Exodus xii. 6,—"And ye shall keep it up until the fourteenth day of the same month: and the whole assembly of the congregation of Israel shall kill it in the evening." "Between the two evenings," is the marginal reading. The Jews divided their afternoon into *two evenings*, viz. from the sixth to the ninth hour, and from the ninth hour to sundown; this, from mid-day to our three o'clock, and from three o'clock to the sun setting. The lamb, which was a type of Christ, was killed in the point in the day we call three o'clock in the afternoon, on the fourteenth of the first month. Was this type exactly fulfilled to our Lord's death? Yes. He was put to death as the Passover, and died at three o'clock, or the ninth hour. See Mark xv. 33—37. Thus the type had an exact fulfilment on the *day*, and at the very *hour*; so exact is God about *time*.

Leviticus xxiii: 9—11,—We read thus, "And the Lord spake unto Moses, saying, Speak unto the children of Israel, and say unto them, When ye be come into the land which I give unto you, and shall reap the harvest thereof, then ye shall bring a sheaf of the first-fruits of your harvest unto the priest; and he shall wave the sheaf before the Lord, to be accepted for you: on the morrow after the Sabbath the priest shall wave it." Here is a type of Christ's resurrection, and Paul tells us, 1st Cor. 15: 20—"But now is Christ risen from the dead, and become the *first-fruits* of them that slept." On what day did our Lord rise from the dead? On the first day of the week, or the "morrow after the Sabbath." Thus exactly fulfilling the type, not only in the *thing* signified, but in *the time*. Lev. xxiii. 15, 16—we have the time of the feast of weeks, or, as it is called, the Pentecost, which signifies the *fiftieth* day. This was the anniversary of the giving of the Law, and the descent of the Lord upon Mount Sinai. Exactly on *that day* did the Holy Spirit descend on the Apostles. Acts ii. 1—4.

If the types *have* been fulfilled exact, as *to time*, even to the *hour*, where that is known, will there not be the same exactness in the fulfilment of those not yet fulfilled? God always has *kept time* in the fulfilment of the prophecies; and thus far, as we have seen, in the types. He will not fail on us now. No, not "one jot or one tittle shall pass from the law till *all* be fulfilled." Let us then look at those types that remain to be accomplished. Lev. xvi. 29—34.— "And *this* shall be a statue for ever unto you, *that* in the seventh month, on the tenth day of the month, ye shall afflict your souls, and do no work at all, *whether* it be *one* of your own country, or a stranger that sojourneth among you: For on that day shall *the priest* make an atonement for you, to cleanse you, *that* ye may be clean from all your sins before the Lord. *It shall be* a Sabbath of rest unto you, and ye shall afflict your souls, by a statue forever. And the priest, when he shall anoint, and whom he shall consecrate to minister in the priest's office in his father's stead, shall make the atonement, and shall put on the linen clothes, *even* the holy garments: And he shall make an atonement for the holy sanctuary, and he shall make an atonement for the tabernacle of the congregation, and for the altar; and he shall make an atonement for the priests, and for all the people of the congregation. And this shall be an everlasting statue unto you, to make an atonement for the children of Israel, for all their sins, once a year." In the 9th chap. we have an account of what was to be done on that day, and at the closing part of it we are told, Lev. ix. 22, 23—"And Aaron lifted up his hand toward the people and blessed them, and came down from offering of the sin-offering, and the burnt offering, and peace-offerings. And Moses and Aaron went into the tabernacle of the congregation, and came out, and blessed the people; and the glory of the Lord appeared unto all the people." Christ, our great High Priest, has gone into the Holy of Holies for us, with his own blood, and "to them that *look for him* shall appear the *second time* without sin unto salvation." Heb. ix. 28. When he comes out of the Holy of Holies, will it not be on the *day* typified? *Beyond a doubt in my mind it will be.* Isaac at this type as set forth in Lev. xxiii. 26, 27, 29, 32 —"And the Lord spake unto Moses saying, Also on the tenth day of the seventh month there shall be a day of atonement: it shall be an holy convocation unto you; and ye shall afflict your souls, and offer an offering made by fire unto the Lord. . . . For whatsoever soul it be that shall be not afflicted in that same day, he shall be cut off from among

CONTENTS

A standing-room only crowd attended the August 1944 centennial service held in the Washington meetinghouse. A special loudspeaker was temporarily installed to accommodate worshipers who had to remain outside during the service. *Photo by T. K. Martin.*

PREFACE

The church at Washington, New Hampshire, represents one of those unusual places in time and place where everything comes together almost as if following a script. Without a doubt the congregation at Washington had a unique influence on the shape of the Seventh-day Adventist Church today. Here several lines of thought converged. The building was constructed by a congregation dedicated to the open-minded search for truth—a dedication that led directly to its acceptance of the Millerite message in 1843 and the Sabbath teaching in 1845. And it was here in the years that followed that the authority of Ellen White's prophetic ministry was convincingly displayed.

Frederick Wheeler, the Methodist circuit rider turned Advent preacher.

The list of those who lived near or worked within this congregation reads like a *Who's Who* of Adventist pioneers: Frederick Wheeler, Rachel Oaks Preston, Joseph Bates, James and Ellen White, Leonard Hastings, Uriah Smith, John Nevins Andrews, and Eugene Farnsworth. At Washington, New Hampshire, the hopes, disappointments, and victories of an entire denomination can be viewed as if in a microcosm. All that is good and right and inspiring about Adventism can be found in its history. If there could be a single birthplace for the Seventh-day Adventist Church, this is the place.

Rachel Oaks Preston introduced Adventists to the seventh-day Sabbath.

The story of the church at Washington, New Hampshire, also teaches us something about our own time. When people open themselves up to the truth and choose to follow it wherever it might lead, no place is too remote and no one is too small or too obscure that God can't use them to shake the world.

New Hampshire, Thy Templed Hills, by Maxfield Parrish, 1936. *Photo courtesy of the Chittenden Bank, Windsor, Vermont.*

CHAPTER 1:

Liberal Principles

In September of 1776 the citizens of a small western New Hampshire settlement called Camden sent a petition to the General Assembly in Exeter to become incorporated as a town. Their appeal read, in part:

> "May it please your honors to incorporate this township by the name of Washington, as in duty bound your honor's most humble petitioners, whose names are underwritten, shall ever pray." [1]

The petition was approved on December 13, and so the town became the first to bear the name of the up-and-coming general, George Washington.

Below: *The Capture of the Hessians at Trenton,* by John Trumbull. George Washington's victory at Trenton, New Jersey, on December 26, 1776, gave the fledgling country its first taste of success in fighting what many believed to be a hopeless battle. *Illustration provided by the Yale University Art Gallery, Trumbull Collection.*

Right: To reach Washington, New Hampshire, Simeon Farnsworth would have taken a route from Massachusetts Bay north through the settlements of Nashua and Hillsborough, a trip totaling just under 100 miles (161 kilometers). *Map by Buster Jackson, Review and Herald Publishing Association.*

One of the petitioners was Simeon Farnsworth, one of the earliest settlers of Washington. His family settled at the foot of Safford Hill, a short distance from the village center.[2]

Like Farnsworth, most of the first residents of Washington came from the region of Massachusetts Bay. They brought with them a love of liberty, a desire for knowledge, and an unwavering faith in God.[3] In the center of the town they built a meetinghouse that served as a government office, a school, and a church. Around this center, the town grew.

Below: The Washington Town Center and the surrounding hills about 1934. *Photo provided by the Washington Historical Society.*

2 Sept 1776

To the General Assembly of New-Hampshire in New-England.

The Petition of the Inhabitants of a certain non incorporated Township, of Land hitherto known by the name of Camden; in the County of Cheshire; in the Government above said

most humbly sheweth

may it please your Honors
That whereas by reason of our being a non-incorporated Township, we are subject to many Inconveniencies, & Disadvantages, as are common, & often incident to non incorporated Societies: both in regard to publick & also our domestick affairs: we therefore your Honors most humble petitioners hereby intreat & implore that according to your wisdom & goodness you would be pleased to remedy the Inconveniencies & Disadvantages to which un-incorporated Towns are liable as such; & to invest this Town with the powers, Liberties & priviledges common to incorporated Towns within this Government; may it please Your Honors to incorporate this Township by the name of Washington ~ ~ and as in duty bound your Honors most Humble Petitioners whose names are under written shall ever pray

Dated at Camden aforesaid September 2d, 1776.

Reuben Kidder	Joseph Rounsevil	William Steel
John Safford	Benja Babcock	Archd White
Jacob Burbank	Josiah Prockter	Robert Mann
David Danforth	John Steel	James Maxwel
William Procter	Samuel Copeland	Jonathan Prockey
Nathan Procter	Abner Sampson	Ephraim Severane
Eben Spauling	Daniel Severane	Simeon Farnsworth
William White	David Lowell Junr	Archd White Junr
David Lowell	Simeon Lowell	Peter Lowell
Lemuel Faber	James Copeland	Paul Hale
Church Faber		Jacob Copeland

The signature of Simeon Farnsworth on the Camden petition of incorporation, 1776. Simeon was born in 1746, the great-grandson of Matthias Farnsworth, who arrived in Groton, Massachusetts, back in 1664. Simeon's move to New Hampshire likely preceded his marriage to Esther Ellinwood, a resident of Lyndeborough, which was only 35 miles (57 kilometers) southeast of present-day Washington. Their first child, a daughter, was born in 1773. *Photo provided by the New Hampshire state archives.*

In 1785 a dispute over the location of the Washington Town House arose between residents living to the southwest of Washington around Millen Pond and those living to the northeast around Lovell Mountain. The general court sent a delegation to decide the issue, with the result that the Town House was built in the center of town in 1787. The bell tower wasn't added until the 1820s. *Meetinghouse drawing courtesy of Ronald and Grace Jager, in* Portrait of a Hill Town *(1977), p. 471.*

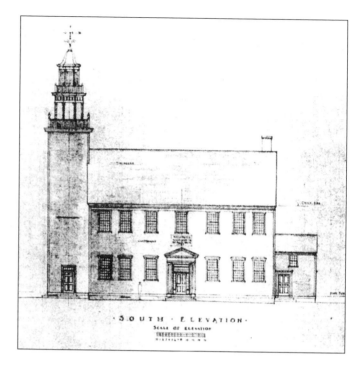

· S O U T H · E L E V A T I O N ·

Below: In *A Sacred Deposit,* p. 68, historian Ron Jager notes that the bell in the Washington Town House tower was cast in 1826 at the George Handel Holbrook Foundry in East Medway, Massachusetts. Holbrook, whose family was noted for its musical ability, learned metalworking at the famous Revere Foundry but left, it is said, because he could not bear the off-key tone of Revere bells. A long-held tradition has it that to sweeten the tone of the Washington bell, 20 silver dollars were mixed into the metal before it was cast—a practice widely accepted though never proven effective. *Photo by Joshua Rodman.*

Above: The 700-pound (318-kilogram) bell hangs from a frame supported under the belfry floor by a pair of 17-inch (43-centimeter) cross beams, two of the largest in the Town House. The bell rope can be seen passing through on the right. *Photo by Joshua Rodman.*

By 1839 Washington had grown to the point that members of the Congregational First Parish Society, the dominant congregation in the town, set about to build a new church in the town center. They intended that the building would be shared by other Christian groups in the town, with some exceptions.

Daniel Farnsworth.
Photo courtesy of the Ellen G. White Estate.

The Proprietors' constitution said: "Each member shall have the right to claim and hold the Meeting House for Orthodox Congregational or Presbyterian preaching against all other claims.' . . . 'Restorationists' were excluded by name, . . . [as were those contrary] 'to Orthodox sentiments now generally understood.' "[4]

This exclusive plan was opposed by the Christian Brethren, a small separatist group that included men such as John Stowell, Newell Mead, and Daniel Farnsworth, the youngest son of Simeon. The

The Washington Town Center about 1860. Fifty years after the Town House was built, the old contest between north and south played out once more when plans for a new church were made, with the grandchildren of the original residents taking sides again. The decision on where to build dragged out for almost a decade. When at last the plan was finalized in 1839, many of those on the losing side withdrew and began meeting in private homes around Millen Pond. *Photo provided by the Washington Historical Society.*

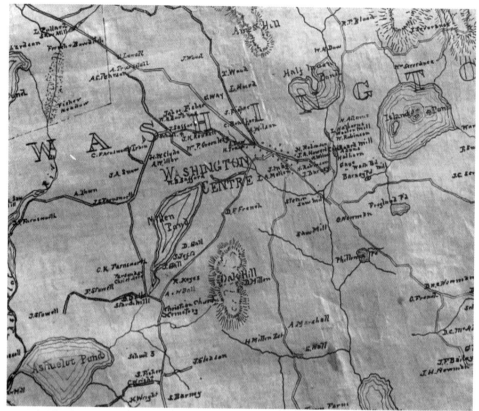

A hand-drawn map of Washington from about 1854. Millen Pond was a natural reservoir to the south and west of the town, part of a water system used by the many mills around Washington. Those residents living near it primarily worked small farms, and formed a close-knit community of their own. It was from this community that the founding members of the Washington Meeting House were drawn. *Photo provided by the Washington Historical Society.*

Brethren had ties to the Christian Connection, a loose-knit confederation of churches that represented perhaps the first indigenous religious movement in America.[5] As a rule they were suspicious of organized religion and encouraged members to take religious destiny into their own hands and to think for themselves. While they were tenacious in their own beliefs, they did not force their beliefs on others; rather, they were willing to give every man the utmost freedom of thought and expression.[6] To the Christian Brethren, the restrictions imposed by the First Parish Society suggested that its members were closing their minds as well as the doors of the meetinghouse.

Left: Construction techniques in the 1840s involved a great deal of hand labor. These same techniques were scrupulously observed in the reconstruction of a barn in Old Sturbridge Village, Massachusetts, in the late 1980s.
Photo provided by the Old Sturbridge Village Visual Resource Library.

But the Christian Brethren could not prevail. Reluctantly they withdrew from the First Parish Society. In 1842 they bought a small plot of land some distance from the new Congregationalist structure in the center of town. It was in an area known as the Barney neighborhood; the widow of Timothy Barney[7] donated the purchase price of $5.[8] Here they built their own meetinghouse.

Below: Barn raising in the late 1980s at Old Sturbridge Village, Massachusetts.
Photo provided by the Old Sturbridge Village visual resource library.

Frederick Wheeler, about 1860. Wheeler was born in Acton, Massachusetts, in 1811, the son of a Captain Theodore Wheeler. He was evidently living in the Washington area by 1832 when, at the age of 21, he married the daughter of a prominent Washington farmer, William Proctor. By 1840 Wheeler was an ordained minister of the Methodist Episcopal Church and became its circuit rider serving congregations in Washington and Hillsborough. *Photo provided by the Review and Herald Publishing Association.*

F. WHEELER.

"The Society which call themselves Christian Brethren calculate to act upon liberal principles . . . they never calculate to assume the ground that they are infallible or too pure to unite with other societies in their worship that try to love and serve God, much less to shut out any society whatever that wishes to occupy our houses of worship when not occupied by us." [9]

The construction took about six weeks [10] and, when completed, the one story meetinghouse was only 30 feet wide and 40 feet long. [11] The Brethren secured young Frederick Wheeler, a recently ordained Methodist circuit rider living in nearby Hillsboro, to be their pastor. Wheeler, just 31 years old, was already known in the town, having married the daughter of a prominent Washington citizen almost a decade before.[12]

By 1842 this small congregation had demonstrated they would follow God's direction wherever it might lead. And their faithfulness was soon to be tested.

The Washington Meeting House was built on land once used for farming. In the 1840s it would have been surrounded by cleared fields rather than the thick forest seen today. *Photo provided by the Review and Herald Publishing Association.*

Hieroglyphic of a Christian, by an unknown artist about 1850. Religious fervor was common in New England during the early 1800s, opening the way for many religious movements, including Millerism. *From the Eleanor and Mabel Van Alstyne American Folk Art Collection, Smithsonian National Museum of American History.*

CHAPTER 2:

Millerites

The years following American independence saw increased spiritual fervor in Washington, as well as throughout all New England. The sense of anxiety that hovered over the region increased as what were taken to be ominous signs appeared in the heavens.

Late in the afternoon of May 9, 1780, New England was cast into an almost suffocating darkness that lasted the better part of three days. The sun, when visible at all, appeared a deep red and was said to have looked like a clotter of blood. The *Boston Gazette* reported flashes in the sky like the aurora borealis. And ships off the coast of Massachusetts

James and Sarah Tuttle, 1836 by Joseph H. Davis. Provided by the New York Historical Society.

Above: In the spring of 1843 a large comet arched through the heavens of New England, which was regarded as the most marvelous of any on record up to that time. The comet was clearly seen with the naked eye, having been observed in the daytime before it was visible at night. Many Millerites believed it to be a harbinger of the soon-coming destruction of the world. *Engraving from* Our First Century; *1776-1876.*

Frederick Douglass was a teenage house servant in Baltimore, Maryland, when he witnessed the falling of the stars on November 13, 1833. *Photo provided by the National Portrait Gallery.*

were forced to steer by candlelight.[1]

It was followed on November 13, 1833, by the largest meteor shower in recorded history. "Probably no celestial phenomena has ever occurred in this country," wrote Denison Olmsted, an astronomer at Yale, ". . . [that] was viewed with so much admiration and delight by one class of spectators, or with so much astonishment and fear by another."[2]

Left: Portrait of Abraham Davenport by Ralph Earl, 1788. During the Dark Day of March 1780, members of the Connecticut House of Representatives in Hartford feared the end of the world was upon them and made a motion to adjourn. Colonel Abraham Davenport from Stamford would not go along. "The day of judgment is either approaching, or it is not," he said. "If it is not, there is no cause for an adjournment; if it is, I choose to be found doing my duty." The council adjourned anyway. *Illustration courtesy of Yale University Art Gallery. Gift of John A. Davenport, B.A., 1926.*

Below: The Great Dark Day of 1780, followed by the falling of the stars in 1833, brought vividly to the minds of New Englanders the imagery of Matthew 24:29: "The sun will be darkened, and the moon will not give its light; the stars will fall from the sky, and the heavenly bodies will be shaken" (NIV). In such a setting the Millerite message found ready acceptance. *Illustration provided by Aurora University Library.*

William Miller did not consider himself well educated, nor much of a public speaker. For several years, early in his study of biblical prophecy, he could not escape the distinct possibility that he might be wrong. *Illustration provided by the Ellen G. White Estate.*

Abolitionist Frederick Douglass commented, "I witnessed this gorgeous spectacle, and was awe-struck. . . . I was not without the suggestion, at the moment, that it might be the harbinger of the coming of the Son of Man; . . . I was prepared to hail Him as my friend and deliverer. I had read that the 'stars shall fall from heaven,' and they were now falling. . . . I was looking away to heaven for the rest denied me on earth." [3]

One of those who believed that he saw the beginning of the end was William Miller, a respected farmer and former militia officer living in Low Hampton, New York. Once an avowed deist, Miller had come to make the Bible the center of his life. The prophecies of Daniel in particular intrigued him, and he spent years searching out their meaning. In 1818 his tireless study brought him to the staggering conclusion that Jesus Christ would return to the earth, personally and visibly, by 1843—only 25 years away. He wrote:

> "I could at first hardly believe the result to which I had arrived; but the evidence struck me with such force that I could not resist my convictions. I became nearly settled in my conclusions, and began to wait, and watch, and pray for my Savior's coming." [4]

William Miller's house in Low Hampton, New York, about 1895. *Photo provided by the Review and Herald Publishing Association.*

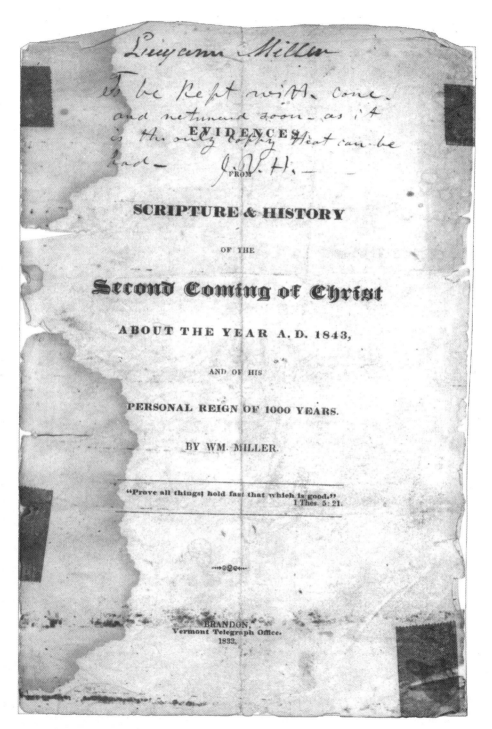

Title page of William Miller's first 64-page pamphlet published in Brandon, Vermont, in 1833. *Photo provided by the Andrews University Heritage Room.*

It was such an incredible proposition, even to Miller, that it took more than 12 years before he could work up the courage to present his ideas publicly. In 1831 Miller cautiously began to meet with small groups, here and there, throughout New England. At first few people were interested, but when the stars began to fall his belief in a soon-coming apocalypse seemed confirmed.[5]

By 1842 Miller had presented more than 4,500 lectures to more than a half million listeners.[6] Newspapers picked up on the story too. Horace Greeley took time out from his ongoing battle for abolition to devote an entire issue of the New York *Tribune* to Miller's prophetic interpretations. And then debunked them.[7]

Born on a hardscrabble New Hampshire farm and apprenticed to a Vermont printer at age 15, Horace Greeley worked his way to prominence as founding editor of the New York *Tribune,* one of the first "penny daily" newspapers. In addition to the daily *Tribune,* Greeley published a weekly edition that reached at its height nearly a million readers throughout the United States and western territories, and which gave the celebrated and eccentric editor an enormous influence on American popular opinion, particularly on the issue of slavery and its abolition. Horace Greeley portrait by Matthew Brady, about 1860. *Photo provided by the Library of Congress.*

New York *Tribune Extra,* March 2, 1843. The enthusiasm for the Millerite message prompted Horace Greeley and the editors of the New York *Tribune* to publish a special issue dedicated to pointing out their objections to Miller's teachings. In many quarters it may have actually encouraged the believers. *Illustration provided by the Loma Linda University Heritage Room.*

View of New Bedford Harbor in 1857 by Joseph F. A. Cole. New Bedford lay directly across the Acushnet River from Fairhaven, and later became an industrial center. This is a view Joseph Bates would have been familiar with. *Illustration courtesy of the New Bedford Free Public Library.*

Joseph Bates at age 26, by an unknown artist. *Photo provided by the Del. E. Webb Memorial Library, Loma Linda, California.*

But Miller's following continued to grow. Called "Millerites," or sometimes "Adventists," they numbered in the hundreds of thousands. Perhaps a dozen independent papers sprang up in New England to help tell the news. *The Signs of the Times,* the most influential Millerite publication, reached an estimated 50,000 readers.[8] Another paper, *The Hope of Israel,* found its way to Fairhaven, Massachusetts, where Joseph Bates, a retired sea captain-turned-Christian Connection minister, was vigorously spreading the word.[9] He was undaunted by the disbelief he met, even from his own family. In a letter to his sister he acknowledges her skepticism:

> "'O', say you, 'I can't believe it. Joseph must be crazy.' I feel and believe that I am coming to my senses. O what a tremendous hour this will be to the wicked. Let us see to it, my dear sister, that we are prepared for that eventful hour."[10]

In *Trumpeter of Doomsday* H. A. Larrabee said, "What Miller added to the traditional fire-and-brimstone mixture was the ingredient of mathematical computation as an 'infallible' method of unraveling mysterious prophecies. This appealed strongly to Yankee ingenuity, and challenged the competitive

Cover of an issue of *Signs of the Times* from April 15, 1841. *Illustration provided by The Ellen G. White Estate.*

The camp meeting was a prominent institution of the American frontier. It originated in 1800 under the preaching of James McGready in Kentucky early in the course of a religious revival. Camp meetings soon spread throughout the United States. Immense crowds, bringing bedding and provisions in order to camp on the grounds, flocked to hear noted revivalist preachers. William Miller was the featured speaker at many such camp meetings during the 1830s and 1840s. *Illustration provided by the Review and Herald Publishing Association.*

spirit of thousands of amateur Bible-interpreters. In addition, he laid great stress upon the imminent casting down of the mighty, the wealthy, and the educated from their exalted seats, and the raising up of the weak and humble and faithful to replace them. More than that, in an age of competing utopias, when reformers were sprouting everywhere and promising everything . . . Miller outbid them all." [11]

"Miller's theory is *all moonshine,*" retorted the Reverend Dr. Sharp. [12]

The Millerites pressed on. Circuit-riding preachers carried the message from town to town, and people flocked to hear them. Local pastors welcomed the

W. Withers,
Bastine

THE
SERMONS, DOCTRINES,

AND

PECULIAR VIEWS

OF

THE MILLERITES,

AS PREACHED BY

FATHER MILLER AND HIS BRETHREN,

MESSRS, HIMES, LITCH, FITCH, &c.,

IN

THE BIG TENT AT NEWARK,

November, 1842,

WHEREIN THEY ATTEMPT TO PROVE, FROM THE PROPHECIES OF SCRIPTURE, THAT

The World will be Destroyed in 1843.

ALSO,

Dr. Brownlee's Sermon,

IN REPLY TO FATHER MILLER,

WHEREIN HE ATTEMPTS TO PROVE THAT THE MILLENNIUM WILL NOT COMMENCE BEFORE 1866.

NEW YORK:

Published at the Herald Office, Northwest Corner of Fulton and Nassau Streets.

1842.

Title page of a collection of sermons given by several Millerite leaders at the Newark, New Jersey, camp meeting in November 1842, accompanied by William C. Brownlee's rebuttal. The collection was published by the New York *Herald. Courtesy of Aurora University Library.*

Rural Post Office (1857), by Thomas Pritchard Rossiter. In the mid-1800s the farmer's main link to the outside world was the post office. Getting the mail often required a full day's travel, round-trip. It was doubtless a social event as well, giving isolated families a chance to catch up on news and information. *Photograph provided by Superstock.*

boost in their attendance, but more often than not they themselves refused to accept it.

In 1842 Joshua Goodwin, a minister from Maine,[13] brought the Advent teaching to Washington, New Hampshire. It is possible that Joseph Bates accompanied him.[14] True to their constitution, the Christian Brethren opened the doors of their meetinghouse to them. Goodwin's presentations stirred their hearts as nothing else had. By the spring of 1843 the entire congregation had accepted the

Joshua Goodwin's son Jasper (**above, left**) was born in Dartmouth, Massachusetts, in 1849. His mother, Harriet Mead Goodwin, whom Joshua married in 1843, was the sister of William Farnsworth's wife, Sarah, and Newell Mead, both living in Washington. When Joshua died in 1851, Harriet and her young son moved back to Washington, where Jasper grew up to become a prominent citizen, financing a number of ambitious projects in the town. **Above, right:** Jasper Goodwin, seated at center, relaxes in 1891 with guests on the front porch of the Lovell House, a Washington hotel he owned. *Photos provided by the Washington Historical Society.*

Above: Portland, Maine, 1848. *Photo provided by the Maine Historical Society.*
Below, right: Robert Harmon, the father of Ellen Gould Harmon, was a deacon at the Pine Street Methodist Church in Portland, Maine, when he first heard William Miller preach at the nearby Casco Street church in March 1840. *Photo provided by the Ellen G. White Estate.*

Advent message. Frederick Wheeler, who had learned of Miller's teaching through published sermons, also became a devoted adherent.[15]

That summer another young Millerite preacher named James White set out from Palmyra, Maine, on an evangelistic tour that would eventually take him as far as Portland. A member of the Christian Connection since age 15,[16] he had been a Millerite for less than a year, but already the 21-year-old White had led nearly 1,000 people to accept the Advent message. Later, while working in Portland, he met the 16-year-old daughter of Robert Harmon, the local hatmaker. Her name was Ellen.[17]

The young woman in the photograph above is believed to be Rachel Delight Oaks, the daughter of Rachel Oaks Preston, taken sometime before 1858 when Delight suddenly fell ill and died. The photograph is identified only as Rachel Oaks, but because both the mother and the daughter were named Rachel, it is not clear which of the two she might be. Analysis of the mother's one known surviving portrait (see p. 38) and this one suggest the woman pictured is Rachel Delight, the daughter. *Photo provided by Robert Reed.*

CHAPTER 3:

Sabbathkeepers

In 1843 Delight Oaks moved from Verona, New York, to Washington, New Hampshire, to take charge of a public school there. Still a teenager, she rented a room from Cyrus Farnsworth, a son of Daniel, and attended services with his family in the Washington meetinghouse. Shortly before Thanksgiving her mother arrived.[1]

Rachel Oaks Preston was 34 years old when she came to Washington. A widow for several years, she had recently married Robert Preston, a descendant of a Revolutionary family in Massachusetts.[2] Like her daughter, Rachel was a Seventh Day Baptist, an organization devoted to the literal application of the

Below: The Penniman School, built in 1827, was typical of the one-room rural schools in which Delight Oaks might have taught. In *Portrait of a Hill Town,* page 107, Jager reports that the school was partially funded through an 1817 bequest of $500 made by Squire Thomas Penniman, who was noted both for his generosity and for his potato whiskey still. *Photo provided by the Washington Historical Society.*

fourth commandment. And she brought with her a strong desire to share her beliefs. Perhaps in response to the general excitement of the times, her church had launched the most aggressive evangelistic campaign in its history. In the fall of 1843 the Seventh Day Baptists voted:

> "In view of the imperious duty devolving on us to publish the truth of God to the world, it is advisable to make an appeal to the various orders of Christians, in reference to the Sabbath of the Bible; urging them to a thorough examination of the subject, as one of great importance to the cause of God." [3]

The enthusiasm for Jesus' return exhibited by the Advent believers in Washington did not move

Rachel Oaks, a widow, married Nathan Preston in 1843, the same year she moved to New Hampshire to be with her daughter. It is not known if her husband accompanied her there; although a number of property owners by the name of Preston are listed in census records of the time, none have the first name of Nathan. *Photo provided by the Ellen G. White Estate.*

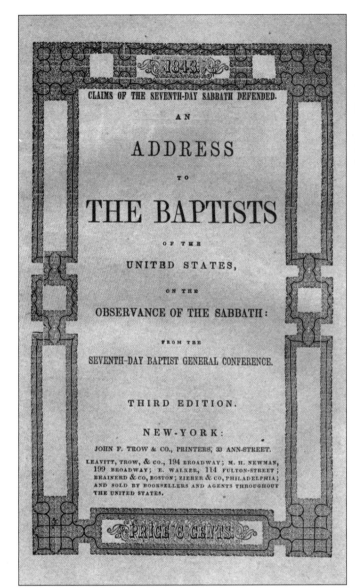

Above: Thomas Brown was the principal writer of the letter of understanding sent out by the Seventh Day Baptist General Conference to other denominations in 1843. The son of a Sundaykeeping Baptist minister, Brown was uniquely suited to make this appeal, having passed through his own personal struggle over accepting the Sabbath in 1839.
Left: A Seventh Day Baptist Sabbath tract from 1843.
Photos provided by Don A. Sanford, historian at the Seventh Day Baptist Historical Society, Janesville, Wisconsin.

Rachel. She was certain in her own mind that the Lord was not coming to translate a company of people who were openly breaking His commandment of seventh-day worship. The Millerite Adventists, on the other hand, thought her views a distraction from the all-important message of the Advent.[4]

Though Rachel was a Sabbathkeeper, she attended services at the meetinghouse on Sundays also, perhaps partly for the companionship of other

In many churches common cups were used for communion services. These pieces are typical of ones used by Methodist congregations in the 1840s.
Photo provided by the General Commission of Archives and History, United Methodist Church.

Christians, and partly to await an opportunity to advocate her beliefs.

Her opportunity came one Sunday morning in early 1844 as Frederick Wheeler prepared to conduct a Communion service in the meetinghouse. Standing before the table near the front of the church, he said that anyone wishing to participate in the Lord's Supper must be keepers of God's commandments. Out in the congregation Rachel could hardly keep her seat. A few days later she approached Wheeler.

"I came near getting up in the meeting at that point and saying something," she told him.

"What was it you had in mind to say?" he asked.

"I wanted to tell you that you would better set that Communion table back and put the cloth over it, until you begin to keep the commandments of God [yourself]"[5]

This pulpit is believed to have been the one used by Frederick Wheeler during the 1840s and 1850s when the Sabbathkeepers moved from the meetinghouse to private homes. The economical design provided for both preaching and administration; the drawers served as a portable church office, where the record books and church papers could be stored. *Photo by Joshua Rodman, courtesy Washington Historical Society.*

Left: James K. Polk squared off against Henry Clay in the presidential election of 1844. Polk campaigned on the theme of "54-40 or Fight," referring to the disputed border of the Oregon territory. It is unlikely many of the Millerites paid much attention to the presidential race since they fully expected that by the time it was held there would be no nation over which to preside. As it turned out, there was, and Polk did. *Illustration provided by the Library of Congress.*

Wheeler was surprised. He resolved to study the Sabbath commandment and its meaning for himself, starting with several Seventh Day Baptist tracts Rachel had brought with her from New York. And he was persuaded. By the end of March he publicly announced his intention to obey all the commandments, including the fourth.[6] His Washington Adventist congregation, however, remained unconvinced.

William Miller expected Jesus to return sometime between March 21, 1843, and March 21, 1844, though he also allowed the possibility for a slight error in his computations. When the year came and went without incident, the Millerites were disappointed but not despondent.[7] They continued in the

Below: Samuel Morse sent history's first telegram from his desk in Washington, D.C., to an associate 40 miles (64 kilometers) away in Baltimore, Maryland, on May 24, 1844.

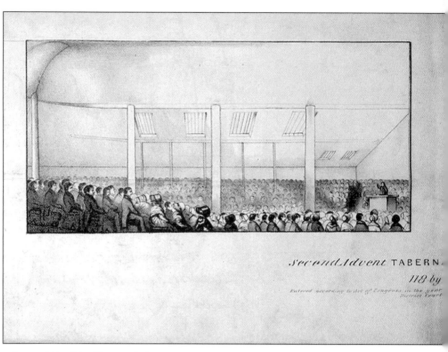

Above and top right: The Boston Tabernacle was a huge wooden building designed to hold up to 10,000 people. It was built in 1843 under the direction of Joshua Himes for the purpose of providing William Miller with a venue as big as his message. Here, Miller made several presentations on the Advent and where Samuel Snow captivated his audience with the date of October 22. The Tabernacle burned in 1846 and was replaced by the Howard Athenaeum. *Illustration provided by the General Conference of Seventh-day Adventists' Office of Archives and Statistics.*

firm, though now indefinite, conviction that the return of Jesus was near.

Miller noted, "The scoffers now will scoff, and say, 'Where is the promise of his coming?' But I must let them scoff; God will take care of me, his truth, and scoffers, too." [8]

But the indefinite soon gave way to a new focus. On July 21, before a congregation in the Boston Tabernacle, a Millerite preacher named Samuel Snow announced that he could identify the very day Jesus would come back. It would coincide, he said, with the biblical Day of Atonement, a holy day the Bible identified as the tenth day of the seventh month. He calculated that in 1844 that day would fall on October 22. [9]

ard St. Boston.

hr in the Clerk's office of the

Deposited March 10th 1843.
John Evans. propy
See Vol. 18, Page 63.

MICROFILMED

Left: Samuel Snow was by turns a Congregationalist, a skeptic, a Millerite minister, and the originator of the "seventh-month movement," a method of interpretation that enabled him to fix October 22, 1844, as the date of Jesus' return. Snow was deeply disappointed when the event did not come to pass, and for a while doubted the prophetic timetable. But he quickly recovered and began advocating new theories that brought him into sharp conflict with the Millerites. Snow shortly fell into extreme fanaticism and finally proclaimed himself to be Elijah the prophet. Soon after, he separated himself from Adventism in every form. *Photo provided by the Ellen G. White Estate.*

Right: On the evening of June 27, 1844, in Carthage, Illinois, a mob broke into the local jail and murdered Joseph Smith, the Mormon leader, and his brother Hyrum, and wounded two others. The four had been arrested for attempting to destroy the press and offices of the Nauvoo *Expositor,* an upstart newspaper critical of Smith and his teachings, particularly polygamy. When it appeared the Smiths would be freed, the mob formed, saying, "If law could not reach them, shot and powder could." *Illustration provided by the Library of Congress.*

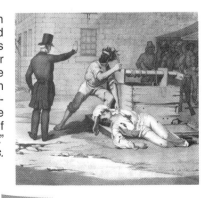

William Miller preaching in the Casco Street Methodist Church, where Ellen Harmon heard the Advent message. *Illustration provided by the Review and Herald Publishing Association.*

Snow had published his ideas as early as February 1843, though few then had paid him any attention. But in the expectant atmosphere that developed after the spring of 1844, his proposition began to take hold. In August Snow presented his ideas at a camp meeting in Exeter, New Hampshire, where the new teaching was heard and accepted by Joseph Bates and James White. It was called the "Midnight Cry." James White noted,

> "The evidences upon which it was based seemed conclusive, and a power almost irresistible attended it. . . . Whatever of differences of opinion . . . were now being swept away and lost sight of in the onward course of this mighty movement." [10]

A sense of certainty settled over the Millerites that inspired them to take determined action. Farmers left their fields, seeing no reason to plant or harvest crops they would never need. Men paid up their debts. Others sold their businesses to help finance a last effort to spread the warning.

"I had some things for sale," said Henry Bear. "When any person came to buy, I would let them have these articles. When they wanted to pay for them I would not receive it, telling them that the world was coming to an end by such a time, and I needed no money as it would do me no good. Of course they sometimes stared at me, astonished.[11]

In New Ipswich, a small town south of Washington, Leonard Hastings decided to leave his potato crop in the ground. "I'll not want them," he said. "The Lord is coming." When his neighbors offered to dig them up for him, he refused. "I'm going to let that field of potatoes preach my faith."[12]

Frederick Wheeler was one of those who sold everything he had to support the cause. His son, George, recalled the situation as follows:

> "Our family, and several others, all moved into the large farmhouse of [my uncle], Washington Barnes, . . . where we all lived together, waiting for the end. I remember how we slept in the attic, and how we children would peek around the blankets they had nailed to the rafters to make partitions between the different families."[13]

Leonard Hastings became a favored friend of James and Ellen White's, hosting them in his home in New Ipswich during many of their trips to New Hampshire. Once, in response to the prayers of Ellen White and others, his wife and infant son were healed of what appeared to be a life-threatening illness. *Leonard Hastings portrait, Ellen G. White Estate.*

MILLERISM. I. T. Hough, tailor and draper, Fifth street, below Market, Philadelphia, has closed his store, and placed the following inscription on his shutters:

> This shop is closed in honor
> of the King of Kings,
> Who will appear about the
> 22d of October.
> Get ready, friends, to crown
> him Lord of all.

A day of thanksgiving is talked of in New Brunswick, for returning solemn thanks for the abundant harvest realized this year, in that province.

Millerites demonstrated their faith in a variety of ways prior to October 22, 1844, including closing their stores, as this newspaper advertisement proclaims. As a result, many Millerites found themselves without a means of support when the time passed. *Photo provided by James Nix.*

"We believed it with our whole souls," said Luther Boutelle. "At no time since 'the day of Pentecost was fully come' had there been the like—a day when Pentecost was so completely duplicated as in 1844, when Adventism prevailed and reigned." [14]

Some gave more than money to the cause. Charles Fitch, an exuberant Millerite preacher from New York, baptized several groups of new believers in Lake Erie on a cold, windy day in late September. His long exposure led to a fever from which he never recovered. He died on October 14. [15]

Above: Buffalo, New York, about 1847. The little lakeside village of Buffalo was transformed by the completion of the Erie Canal in 1825. Within seven years the city's population had doubled to 10,000, and it had become one of the busiest shipping ports in the world. *Engraving provided by Buffalo and Erie County Historical Society.*

Left: Charles Fitch was one of the most fearless, aggressive, and successful Millerite leaders. A former Presbyterian minister, he produced a sensation with his sermons, many of which were reproduced as pamphlets and received broad circulation. Together with Apollos Hale, he designed the widely used 1843 prophetic chart, printed on cloth, which he presented to the Boston General Conference of May 1842. *Portrait provided by the Ellen G. White Estate.*

Left: Joshua V. Himes was, in many respects, the leading figure of the Millerite movement, being responsible for almost single-handedly bringing the message of an obscure country preacher to the attention of the entire country. He launched the *Signs of the Times* with only a dollar in capital, and went on to produce charts, pamphlets, books, tracts, songbooks, broadsides, and handbills—all pointing the reader to the Advent of Christ. *Portrait provided by the Ellen G. White Estate.*
Below: A printing establishment from the 1830s. *Photo provided by Old Sturbridge Village Visual Resource Library.*

In the October 16, 1844, *Advent Herald,* Joshua Himes made this proclamation:

> "As the date of the present number of the *Herald* is our last day of publication before the tenth day of the seventh month, we shall make no provision for issuing a paper for the week following. And as we are shut up to this faith . . . we feel called upon to suspend our labors and await the result. . . . And may we all, with our lamps trimmed and burning, be prepared for His glorious appearing." [16]

"There is something in this present waking up different from anything I have ever before seen," William Miller noted. "The general expression is 'Behold, the bridegroom cometh; go ye out to meet him.' 'Amen. Even so, come, Lord Jesus.'" [17]

The Boston Tabernacle, a well-known Millerite gathering place, is depicted ascending to heaven in this anti-Millerite broadside published in October 1844. Miller himself is shown on the roof, seated on a prophetic chart. The unlucky Joshua Himes is left below, surrounded by bags of money, held down by a forked-tailed devil. *Illustration provided by the Review and Herald Publishing Association.*

CHAPTER 4:

Disappointment

October 22, 1844, passed. Jesus did not come back. Most of the Millerites were devastated. Joseph Bates recalled:

> "You can have no idea of the feeling that seized me. I had been a respected citizen, and had with much confidence exhorted the people to be ready for the expected change. . . . If the earth could but have opened and swallowed me up, it would have been sweetness compared to the distress I felt." [1]

Hiram Edson echoed his distress. "Our fondest hopes and expectations were blasted, and such a spirit of weeping came over us as I never experienced before. It seemed that the loss of all earthly friends could have been no comparison. We wept, and wept, till the day dawn." [2]

Below: The Oxford Street pier in Fairhaven, Massachusetts. In the late 1700s the village of Oxford, at the north end of Fairhaven, was a successful whaling enterprise. But when the first bridge across the Acushnet River was built at the turn of the century, ships were blocked from reaching Oxford. The houses and stores fell into disuse, and the area soon acquired the name "Poverty Point." *Photo provided by the Millicent Library, Fairhaven, Massachusetts.*

Hiram Edson was among the first to understand the true significance of October 22, 1844, or so it appears from the latest research. When the fuller understanding came to the attention of James White and Joseph Bates in 1846, they readily accepted it. Edson sold his farm in Port Byron, New York, to help James White finance the purchase of his first printing press, which was located at Rochester, New York, in 1852. *Portrait provided by the Ellen G. White Estate.*

"It seemed as though all the demons from the bottomless pit were let loose upon us," said William Miller. "The same ones and many more who were crying for mercy two days before were now mixed with the rabble and mocking." [3]

The Millerites now faced a storm of ridicule and scorn. Newspapers derided their disappointment. Stories of Adventists waiting in ascension robes or engaging in other odd behaviors, though untrue, received wide circulation. The attitude was that they had gambled everything and lost. Henry B. Bear lamented:

"This seemed a very tight place to be in: no home to live in, no bed to sleep on, no stove to cook with, no dishes to eat out of, nor anything to put in them, and no Savior to come today, tomorrow or the day after that I know of. A kingdom, it is said, is set up, but where? . . . If when trusting in the scriptures, and praying to God to enlighten, guide and direct me, and I obeying my convictions honestly and faithfully, be deceived and go astray, how could I trust any such being thereafter? I could not. But then, I must trust Him to the end." [4]

Managing a New England farm in the mid-1800s required considerable hand labor in all kinds of weather. Here Henry Shedd, a local pastor, has an impromptu meeting with Nathaniel Cutter near Jaffrey, New Hampshire, in 1869.
Photo provided by the Historical Society, Jaffrey, New Hampshire.

Wagon track on "Minuteman Lane" near Boston, Massachusetts.
Photo courtesy of the New Bedford Free Public Library.

The Millerite movement was not constituted to meet the conditions that confronted it after 1844, and it quickly faded.[5] The Advent believers returned to the lives they thought they had left forever. In Washington, Frederick Wheeler found himself nearly destitute. His son, George, remembered:

> "Father had put everything he had into the cause and when the time passed found himself with less than a dollar, less than a peck of potatoes, not a whole suit of clothes, but his shoes full of holes, with a wife and four children, of whom I was the oldest. . . . Father met a neighbor by the name of Baldwin, who greeted him with 'You didn't go up as you expected. You're still here.'"[6]

George Wheeler in 1936, shortly before his 101st birthday. Though his father was an ardent Seventh-day Adventist believer, George was not. *Photo provided by the Review and Herald Publishing Association.*

Wheeler hired himself out to work as a farmhand and continued to preach in area churches, as he could. Though now a Sabbathkeeper, he went every Sunday for a year to preach at a church in Claremont, New Hampshire, a half day's ride to the north, a service for which he received $4 a week. The next year he did it for free.

The Crops of 1844.

The potatoe crop, which is said to be entirely destroyed by the rot in the whole of northern Vermont, and which is extensively infected all along the Connecticut river valley so near us as Claremont and Newport, we do not as yet learn has been injured much in this part of the valley of the Merrimack. It was remarkable that the rains which here fell about the 7th of September changed all at once the potatoe tops which until that time had been flourishing. Some fields had been previously stricken with rust: whether this last change was the effect of rust or blight, or whether it came in consequence of the ripeness and maturity of the potatoes, we are unable to determine. In several acres of growing potatoes there was every indication of ripeness and maturity while the tops were luxuriant and green: after the rain, the change of tops in these was rapid beyond all previous observation. This change only took place in the crop of white potatoes. A field of three acres of long red potatoes alongside of the whites, with the exception of a dead sprig now and then, remains nearly as green as before the rain. These red potatoes seem to have attained at this time (Sept. 17) nearly or quite their full growth. Some people say these long reds will continue to grow until the frost kills the vines. Should the warm summer continue through the month of September as it has thus far, measuring it by the crop of

The potato blight that struck New England in 1843 and 1844 is thought to have traveled to Europe on trade ships and spread to England and finally to Ireland, where it first infected plants in the southeast. A series of widespread crop failures, beginning in 1846, led to the |greatest loss of life in Irish history. Though records are sketchy, it is believed upwards of 1 million persons died before the disease had run its course four years later. The great migration of Irish farmers escaping what is now known as the great potato famine had a profound impact on the United States. *Illustration provided by the Ellen G. White Estate.*

Leonard Hastings finally dug his potatoes in November. His neighbors, who had so ridiculed his faith a month earlier, were now repentant. A potato blight had struck New England again that season, devastating most of the crop. But the disease affected primarily the harvested potatoes, while those still in the ground escaped. According to tradition, Hastings sold his potatoes that winter for more than 20 times the price of the year before.

In Portland, Maine, Ellen Harmon felt the disappointment as keenly as anyone. She had been an invalid for several years, following a childhood accident, and was diagnosed as having tuberculosis while a teenager. By 1844 she was so weak she required almost constant care. With the Advent of Jesus now apparently delayed, Ellen faced an uncertain and, likely, short future.

But her life took a dramatic turn one morning in December when God gave her a vision. Spread out before her were the Advent people, traveling up a narrow path to the City of God, their way illuminated by a light that represented the Midnight Cry message of Christ's soon return. She understood it to mean that, despite all appearances, God had been leading in their 1844 experience and had not abandoned them, as many claimed. Word of her vision spread, and for those who accepted it, the vision offered hope.

To the Remnant Scattered Abroad.

As God has shown me in holy vision the travels of the Advent people to the holy city, and the rich reward to be given to those who wait the return of their Lord from the wedding, it may be my duty to give you a short sketch of what God has revealed to me. The dear saints have many trials to pass through. But our light afflictions, which are but for a moment, will work for us a far more exceeding and eternal weight of glory—while we look not at the things which are seen, for the things which are seen are temporal, but the things which are not seen are eternal. I have tried to bring back a good report and a few grapes from the heavenly Canaan, for which many would stone me, as the congregation bade stone Caleb and Joshua for their report. Num. 14:10. But I declare to you, my brethren and sisters in the Lord, it is a goodly land, and we are well able to go up and possess it.

While praying at the family altar, the Holy Ghost

Otis Nichols at age 75. *Photo provided by the Ellen G. White Estate.*

Ellen Harmon's first vision was written out and published on April 6, 1846. "To the Little Remnant Scattered Abroad," was meant to encourage those Adventists trying to understand what happened in 1844. Otis Nichols, an early believer in Ellen's visions, mailed a copy to William Miller, including on the back a personal appeal inviting him to consider her insights. The broadside was duly received and noted by Miller, though there is no record of any response. *Photo provided by the Review and Herald Publishing Association.*

Facing page: By December 1844 Ellen Harmon was not expected to live much longer. Diagnosed with "dropsical consumption" —most probably tuberculosis—she was almost unable to breathe and coughed up mouthfuls of blood. To relieve the strain of caring for Ellen, family friends brought her into their homes for short periods. During one such stay with Elizabeth Haines in south Portland, Ellen experienced her first vision. *Painting by Harry Anderson. Art provided by the Review and Herald Publishing Association.*

Miller, his health weakened by the strenuous years of traveling and preaching, retired to his home in Low Hampton, New York.

"My hope in the coming of Christ is as strong as ever. . . . I have fixed by mind upon another time, and here I mean to stand until God gives me more light. And that is Today, Today, and TODAY, until He comes.[7]

He died on December 20, 1849.[8]

Above: In 1848 William Miller built this small chapel on his farm in Low Hampton, New York, for the small local company who remained loyal "Adventists" though holding to no specific timetable. A century after Miller's death the building came into the possession of the Advent Christian Church, Sunday-keeping descendants of the Millerite movement, who retain ownership of the chapel to this day. *Photo provided by the Ellen G. White Estate.*

Left: Elder J. E. Edwards and Mrs. Ella Adams, granddaughter of William Miller, stand beside a plaque commemorating the chapel's heritage in August 1960. *Photo by M. Rees.*

William Miller died on December 20, 1849. He was 67 years old. At his bedside was Joshua Himes (left) who, 20 years before, had made a solemn pact to take Miller's message to the entire country and beyond, which he did beyond all expectations. Miller's gravestone (above), less than one mile (1.6 kilometers) from his home in Low Hampton, New York, has engraved upon it the words "At the Time Appointed the End Shall Be." Ellen White wrote of Miller, "Angels watch the precious dust of this servant of God, and he will come forth at the sound of the last trump" (*Early Writings*, p. 258).
Miller tombstone photo, Ellen G. White Estate.

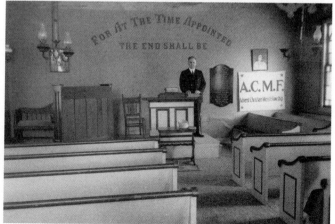

Above: After 1844 Miller's timetable for the Advent of Christ is reflected on the words now stenciled on the front wall of the chapel: "For at the Time Appointed, the End Shall Be." *April 1945 photo provided by the Review and Herald Publishing Association.*

William Farnsworth fathered 22 children, creating a family situation for which Ellen White rebuked him. She testified that he had increased his family without realizing the responsibility, and that the burdens he'd placed on his first wife had led to her death. "Your present wife has a hard lot," White wrote. "Her vitality is nearly exhausted. You have not done your duty to your children, but have left them to grow up in ignorance" (*Testimonies,* vol. 2, p. 94). *Photo provided by the Review and Herald Publishing Association.*

CHAPTER 5:

"What's the News?"

The disappointment of 1844 had a lasting effect on the people of New England. Many former Millerites left their churches and never went back, determined, as they put it, not to be fooled again. Others were more thoughtful. Their resolve to understand the Bible only increased with the passing of time. In Washington one such person was William Farnsworth.

William Farnsworth turned 37 years old in 1844.[1] The eldest son of Daniel, he made his living as a farmer. He was big, a head taller than most of his neighbors, and reputed to be the strongest man in the county. In the course of a long life he married twice and fathered 22 children. John, the eldest son, was 40 years old when his youngest brother, Merton, was born.[2]

The home of William Farnsworth shortly before its demolition in 1974.
Photo provided by the Ellen G. White Estate.

John Farnsworth **(above),** the oldest son of William, was 40 years old when his youngest brother, Merton **(below),** was born.
Photos provided by the Ellen G. White Estate.

Cyrus Farnsworth, the fifth son of Daniel and younger brother to William, married 21-year-old Delight Oaks, the new school-teacher who rented a room in his home. Together they had three sons before Rachel died unexpectedly in 1858. *Photo provided by James Nix.*

William Farnsworth was also a leader. President of the Christian Society at the time the Washington meetinghouse was built, he was, in 1843, one of the first to accept the Millerite message.[3] He soon became acquainted with Rachel Oaks Preston and her ideas about the Sabbath. And by the end of 1844 he was ready to lead again.[4] S. N. Haskell writes:

"One Sunday during the service, one member got up and said he had been studying the Bible and was convinced that the seventh day of the week was the Sabbath, instead of the first day, and that he was going to keep it. He was followed by another, and then another, until a small company took their stand to keep the seventh-day Sabbath." [5]

Joining William was his younger brother, Cyrus, and their father, Daniel, and mother, Patty.[6] In the next few weeks Newell Mead followed, as did John Stowell and others. They formed a group of at least 15 that began meeting together in each others' homes, thus leaving the meetinghouse to their former Brethren.[7] Accordingly, their names were crossed out from the list of Christian Brethren in the meetinghouse record book.[8] Wooster Ball, the village blacksmith, who was also the church clerk and kept the record book, scratched his name out with such enthusiasm that it remained barely legible.[9]

Newell Mead was the brother of Sarah Farnsworth and Harriet Goodwin, all prominent players in the Washington story. *Photo provided by the Ellen G. White Estate.*

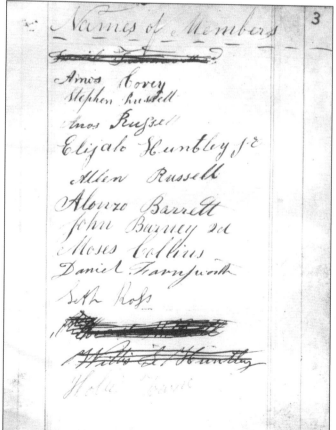

Left: The 1842 clerk book for the Washington, New Hampshire, meetinghouse. Daniel Farnsworth's name is crossed out at the top, and Wooster Ball's name is well-nigh obliterated. **Below:** Worcester Ball, generally referred to as Wooster, had a blacksmith shop on his farm where he specialized in the making of axes. *Photo provided by the Ellen G. White Estate.*

From Washington the Sabbath teaching began to spread. Thomas Preble, the pastor of the Free Will Baptist church in nearby Nashua, and a friend of Frederick Wheeler, also became a Sabbathkeeper. In February 1845 Preble published an article about the Sabbath in *The Hope of Israel*. A short time later it reached the home of Joseph Bates in Fairhaven, Massachusetts.

Thomas Preble was friends with Frederick Wheeler, and as both were Millerites they likely traveled together during Millerite campaigns. It is possible that during one such ride, Wheeler introduced Preble to the seventh-day Sabbath teaching he learned from Rachel Oaks Preston.
Photo provided by the Ellen G. White Estate.

TRACT,

SHOWING THAT THE SEVENTH DAY

SHOULD BE OBSERVED AS THE SABBATH,

INSTEAD OF THE FIRST DAY;

"ACCORDING TO THE COMMANDMENT."

BY T. M. PREBLE.

Remember the Sabbath day to keep it holy. Six days shalt thou labor and do all thy work: But the seventh day is the Sabbath of the Lord thy God: In it thou shalt not do any work, thou, nor thy son, nor thy daughter, thy man-servant, nor thy maid-servant, nor thy cattle, nor thy stranger that is within thy gates; For in six days the Lord made heaven and earth, the sea, and all that in them is, and rested the seventh day: Wherefore the Lord blessed the Sabbath day and hallowed it.—Exodus xx. 8—11.

NASHUA:
PRINTED BY MURRAY & KIMBALL.
1845.

The tract that convinced Joseph Bates of the Sabbath truth was republished in the August 23, 1870, *Advent Review and Sabbath Herald,* a number of years after Preble had, for himself, repudiated the teaching. *Photo provided by the Review and Herald Publishing Association*

Joseph Bates is assumed to have attended Fairhaven Academy, an institution his father helped build in Fairhaven, Massachusetts. Joseph Bates's classroom has been preserved, along with a photograph and citation. *Photo provided by the Review and Herald Publishing Association.*

From the age of 15 Joseph Bates had followed the sea. He had experienced shipwreck, capture, and forced service in the British Navy, and during the War of 1812 he was a prisoner of war in England for two and a half years. After his release he continued his career as a merchant seaman, becoming a captain in 1820. He retired to Fairhaven, Massachusetts, eight years later, having accumulated what was at the time a reasonably small fortune of $11,000.[10]

Joseph Bates became a minister in the Christian Connection movement and, like many Christian ministers, was attracted to the Millerite message.[11] Miller's focus on Scripture and his independent thinking paralleled his own philosophy, and he devoted himself to the movement.

Joseph Bates began practicing temperance even before he became a Christian. He may have been influenced toward this view when a drunken prisoner aroused the guards' attention during an attempt to escape from a British POW ship during the War of 1812. *Photo provided by the Review and Herald Publishing Association.*

Unlike some of his associates, Joseph Bates did not lose faith after the disappointment of 1844. He was convinced that God would give light to His people if they would just wait for it. As he read and reread Preble's article on the seventh-day Sabbath, Bates was sure he had found truth.[12]

"Many things now troubled my mind as to how I could make this great change—family, friends, and brethren; but this one passage of Scripture was, and always will be, as clear as a sunbeam: 'What is that to thee? follow thou me.'"[13]

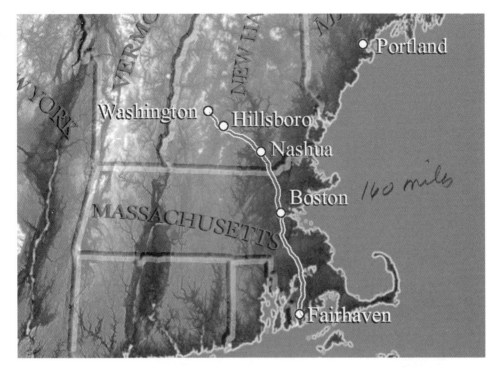

160 miles

Bates was eager to learn more, and in the spring of 1845 he set out for Hillsboro, New Hampshire, where, he had learned, Frederick Wheeler and a small congregation of Sabbathkeepers could be found. Bates arrived at Wheeler's home late at night and, in his eagerness, pounded on the door to wake him.

"Once we heard a racket in the night," George Wheeler remembered later. "Joseph Bates had arrived. . . . They hung up a chart and talked till morning. Then my brother and I and the hired man had to go out and milk 10 or a dozen cows." [14]

Washington, New Hampshire, is 160 miles (257 kilometers) from Fairhaven, Massachusetts, a trip that would have taken Joseph Bates perhaps three days to make. *Map by Buster Jackson, Review and Herald Publishing Association.*

According to George Wheeler, as a 13-year-old boy, he and a hired man took care of a dozen cows on the Wheeler farm. Dairy and livestock were a principle business in New England. *Engraving provided by the Library of Congress.*

Two of the famous maples that stood in front of the Cyrus Farnsworth home were brought down in a storm in 1988.
Photo provided by the Review and Herald Publishing Association.

At dawn Bates and Wheeler traveled to the home of Cyrus Farnsworth in Washington, and the three men sat in the shade of the maples in the front yard and continued their discussion. William Farnsworth lived a short distance down the road, and may well have joined them.[15] The meeting lasted until midday. Then Joseph Bates, having gained what he had come for, set off for home. As he was crossing the Achushnet River Bridge back in Fairhaven, Massachusetts, Bates was met by a friend who called out to him: "Captain Bates, what's the news?" To which Bates replied, "The seventh day is the Sabbath." [16]

Preble's article was reprinted in the form of a tract and distributed throughout New England. In the spring of 1845 it reached John Stowell in Paris, Maine. Stowell, a former Millerite who had sold his farm in anticipation of the Advent, was at the time living with his family in the home of Edward Andrews. At first Stowell laid it aside, but his daughter

Twenty-year-old John Nevins Andrews and his younger brother William, about 1850. John's father, Edward, lost their family farm after the Disappointment of 1844, and by necessity moved in with their friends the Stowells, in Paris, Maine. In 1845, led by the children, both families accepted the Sabbath truth they found in a tract sent to them by Joseph Bates. *Photo provided by the Ellen G. White Estate.*

The Acushnet River bridge was built in 1798 to serve the towns of Fairhaven and New Bedford. The original bridge was destroyed by the Gale of 1869, and rebuilt in 1870. It was replaced by a more modern steel structure in 1898. *Photo provided by the Review and Herald Publishing Association.*

James and Ellen White, with their son Willie, in 1857. *Photo provided by the Ellen G. White Estate.*

THE

SEVENTH DAY SABBATH,

A

PERPETUAL SIGN,

FROM THE BEGINNING, TO THE ENTERING INTO THE
GATES OF THE HOLY CITY,

ACCORDING TO THE COMMANDMENT.

BY JOSEPH BATES.

"Brethren, I write no new commandment unto you, but an old
commandment which ye had from the *beginning.* The old commandment is the WORD which ye have heard from the *beginning*

It was reading Joseph Bates's first tract on the Sabbath that convinced newlyweds James and Ellen White, in the fall of 1846, to keep the Sabbath. A year later Bates had an enlarged and expanded edition printed, financed through an unexpected donation he received when he had but one shilling left of his $11,000 fortune. *Photo provided by the Review and Herald Publishing Association.*

Marian, just 15, was so impressed by its reasoning that she showed it first to her brother, Oswald, then to Andrews' 15-year-old son, John Nevins. Together they resolved to keep the biblical Sabbath. And the next week their families joined them.[17]

In 1846 Joseph Bates published his newfound belief in a 48-page tract entitled *The Seventh-day Sabbath a Perpetual Sign*. He sent a copy to James White, the energetic minister whom he had met earlier, and White's young bride, Ellen. At first the newlyweds were skeptical. But after studying the biblical texts in Bates's tract more carefully, James and Ellen White decided to join the Sabbathkeepers. In April of the following year, while in Topsham, Maine, Ellen had another vision. In it she saw the law of God with a halo of light surrounding the Sabbath commandment, confirming its special significance.[18]

Above: Stockbridge Howland, who opened his Topsham home to James and Ellen White in 1847. *Photo provided by the Review and Herald Publishing Association.*

For a time James White hauled rubble from this work site as it was cut away for a new railroad line between Topsham and Portland, Maine. The pay, however, was unreliable, so he switched to chopping cordwood, for which he earned 50 cents a day. *Photo provided by the Review and Herald Publishing Association.*

James and Ellen White often referred to the home of civil engineer Stockbridge Howland as Fort Howland, an allusion to the owner's steadfast loyalty to the truth. Howland was a prominent citizen of Topsham, Maine, and energetically endorsed the 1844 message. Opponents of Millerism declared that he was neglecting his business and thus was mentally incompetent, and had him placed under legal guardianship. Later, when the county desired a new and superior bridge across the Kennebec River, they called on Howland to do the work. "You know I am not considered competent to attend to my own business," he responded, "and do you come to me to build your bridge?" The county decided that Howland was competent after all, and he built the bridge. *Photo provided by the Review and Herald Publishing Association.*

In July 1847, while James and Ellen White were in Gorham, Maine, expecting the birth of their first child, Henry, the Mormons were following Brigham Young to their new home in what is now Salt Lake City, Utah. Their arrival was reenacted for the camera in 1912. *Photo provided by the Library of Congress.*

On June 14, 1847, Delight Oaks and Cyrus Farnsworth were married.[19] They continued to live in the family home, and together had three sons. In 1858 Delight died, and Rachel Oaks Preston moved back to her native town of Vernon, Vermont. Until the end of her life, Rachel refused to have much to do with the Sabbathkeeping Adventist organization she helped to inspire. She never met Ellen White, but late in life was impressed by her writings and soon changed her attitude. She passed away February 2, 1868. Her last expression was reported to be "Jesus is my friend."[20]

Thomas Preble remained a Sabbathkeeper until the summer of 1847, when, perhaps under the influence of the Sundaykeeping Adventist ministers with whom he associated, he was persuaded to repudiate it.[21] But by that time the message that he had helped advance had taken on a life of its own.

After the unexpected death of her daughter, Delight, in 1858, Rachel Oaks Preston moved back to her hometown of Vernon, Vermont, where she died 10 years later.
Photo provided by the Review and Herald Publishing Association.

An 1893 photograph of veteran Review and Herald workers G. W. Amadon, Oswald Stowell, Warren Bacheller, and Uriah Smith. Warren Bacheller was only 13 years old when he began working the press for James White in Rochester, New York, more than 40 years before. *Photo provided by the Ellen G. White Estate.*

James White used this chart to demonstrate the biblical veracity of the seventh-day Sabbath. He also believed it could make a lovely decoration for the home: "These will be becoming ornaments to the best room of any believing family, and will serve as a happy introduction to the subject of present truth to those who call on them" (*Review and Herald,* Oct. 6, 1863). *Photo provided by the Ellen G. White Estate.*

CHAPTER 6:

New Directions

The visions of Ellen White were becoming more
and more important to the small group of Adventists
who had accepted the visions as being from God.
Though others from the movement claimed to have
received visions and offered various explanations for
the disappointment of 1844, Ellen White's experi-
ences seemed to be of a different order. Even Joseph
Bates, who for many years rejected Ellen's visions, was
finally convinced that her insights revealed more than
human wisdom.[1] And through her influence the
growing faith of the Adventists was given direction.

Most of the stone bridges in the Contoocook River valley near Hillsborough, New
Hampshire, were constructed between 1830 and 1860 by Scotch-Irish settlers, considered
to be the best stonemasons of the period. Built without mortar and sustained only by the
expert shaping of their archstones, these bridges are among the region's most aesthetically
pleasing yet least appreciated landmarks. *Photo provided by Phelps Photo.*

Joseph Bates was still uncertain as to the authority of Ellen White's prophetic insight when, in November 1846, he attended a conference in Topsham, Maine, where Ellen received a vision before his eyes. She described seeing colorful planets surrounded by a number of moons, which Bates, having been trained in astronomy, immediately recognized as Jupiter, Saturn, and Uranus. When Bates learned that Ellen herself had no knowledge of astronomy, he exclaimed, "This is of the Lord." From that day on he accepted Ellen's prophetic gift without reservation. *Photo of Jupiter and its Galilean Satellites provided by NASA.*

Careful Bible study, often prodded by Ellen's prophetic insights, led the believers to understand that the warnings of Miller and others represented the beginning of a great end-time movement symbolized by the three angels of Revelation 14.[2] They saw the Advent teaching and the Sabbath truth as so intertwined that in 1850 James White chose the name *Second Advent Review and Sabbath Herald* for a new paper dedicated to the proclamation of what they now called the three angels' messages.

Joseph Bates from about 1850.
Photo provided by the Review and Herald Publishing Association.

Frederick Wheeler, who had moved from Hillsboro, New Hampshire, to Washington in 1848,[3] wrote the new editor to report the faithfulness of the believers there:

> "There is a little company who have been endeavoring to keep the Sabbath according to the commandment since 1844; and several have lately been led to embrace the truth of the third angel's message in full, and others are more or less interested in the subject."[4]

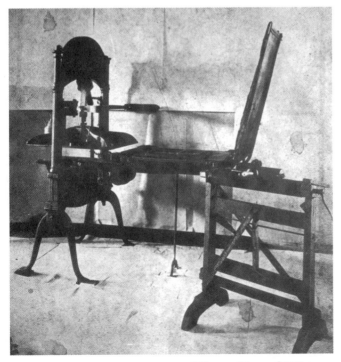

A Washington hand-press was purchased for a little more than $650 and set up in the Whites' house in Rochester. James White bought $2.12 worth of furniture for the house, the first he and Ellen could call their own. The first issue of the *Review* to be printed on the new press appeared on May 27, 1852.
Photo provided by the Review and Herald Publishing Association.

This report aroused the interest of James White.[5] In January 1851 he and Ellen visited what was, in fact, America's first Sabbathkeeping Adventist congregation.[6] James wrote, "They have but recently embraced the message of the third angel, yet they are decided and strong. Our dear Brother Wheeler, of Washington, told us, with much feeling, that he felt deeply impressed with a sense of duty to go out and give the message. We hope the way will soon open before our brother, so that he may go out."[7]

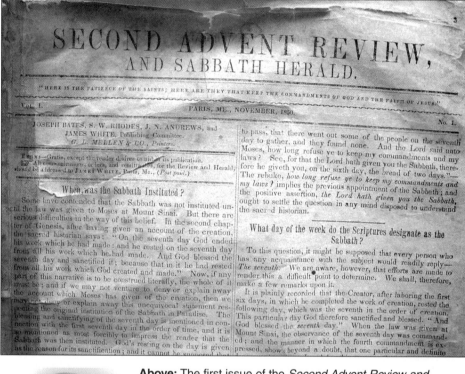

Above: The first issue of the *Second Advent Review and Sabbath Herald* was dated November 1850 and was published in Paris, Maine. *Photo provided by the Ellen G. White Estate.*
Left: Oswald Stowell was one of the first men to run a press for the Review and Herald. Once, while working in Rochester, New York, he fell ill, and his physician gave him up for dead. A number of the believers prayed for his healing; he was back at work in two days. *Photo provided by the Ellen G. White Estate.*

James and Ellen White in Battle Creek, Michigan, 1864. *Photo provided by the Ellen G. White Estate.*

Perhaps in response to Wheeler's enthusiasm, several conferences were held in Washington during succeeding years, and the number of new believers in the area grew. In October 1851 James and Ellen White conducted meetings, during which seven deacons were set apart for the purpose of caring for the poor in the community, and so heralded the beginning of a church organization.[8]

At one of these meetings, held in the farmhouse of John Stowell during October 1851, Ellen was given a vision.[9] George Wheeler tells what he saw:

"While [we were] out doing chores, they came running out to say that Mrs. White was in vision, and we all hurried in. I stood up on a chair so I could see. She was lying down on a bed and talking, and remained in vision about half an hour. Then she threw down her hands and got up."[10]

Not all who witnessed Ellen's vision that day were convinced it was of God. Perhaps her most vocal critic in Washington was Stephen Smith. Though a longtime member, he was not considered a friendly man. He had a quick temper and blistering tongue that he did not hesitate to use.

The Town Center of Washington, New Hampshire, about 1895, showing the Town House, school, Congregational church, and the Lovell house. As white paint was expensive, it was often used on only those parts of a building visible from the main road. A reddish brown coating derived from iron oxide was used on the rest, as can be seen in this view of the Town House. *Photo provided by the Washington Historical Society.*

Stephen Smith was a hard-bitten New Englander who liked nothing better than a good squabble. He often said he liked coming to church to "rap on the hive to hear the bees hum." His distrust of Ellen White was deep, and even witnessing her experience a vision was not enough to convince him that she was inspired of God. *Photo provided by the Ellen G. White Estate.*

Ernest Farnsworth says of him: "When I was a lad he used to come to the Washington church to blow off steam. As he put it, to rap on the hive and hear the bees hum. He was so loud and vicious in his talks that we youngsters were afraid of him. But in a testimony meeting, everyone was permitted to speak, and so [he did].[11]

Smith seemed particularly receptive to the various movements that sprouted from the Millerite experience, advocating first one idea, then another, until no one quite knew what he believed. But regarding Ellen White he was clear: she was a fraud, and he would have nothing to do with her.

What Stephen Smith saw at the Stowell house that day did not change his mind. If anything, it only seemed to harden his opposition. His critical spirit

Ernest Farnsworth at age 75. *Photo provided by the Ellen G. White Estate.*

became so disruptive that before the conference closed that October, he was officially separated from the congregation at Washington.[12]

In September 1852 another conference was held in Washington, with James White once more attending. For the first time the word "lukewarm," the condition of the Laodicean church of Revelation 3, was applied to Sabbathkeeping Adventists, perhaps reflecting the general spiritual condition of the membership there.

Folk art representing a nineteenth-century church meeting. *Abby Aldrich Rockefeller Folk Art Museum, Williamsburg, Virginia.*

Sitting out in the congregation was Uriah Smith, a promising young student from Phillips Academy in nearby Exeter.[13] Smith, the son of a former Millerite, had grown up in the town of West Wilton, a short day's ride from Washington. After the disappointment of 1844 he showed little interest in formal religion. His older sister, Annie, however, was more open. In 1851, while in school in Boston, she attended a series of meetings held by

Left: When Uriah Smith was a boy, an infection brought on by an illness required the amputation of his left leg above the knee. Dr. Amos Twitchell, from nearby Keene, New Hampshire, cut off the leg without the benefit of anesthetic, while his mother and sister held him down. The operation took 20 minutes. *Photo provided by the Review and Herald Publishing Association.*

Below: At age 16 Uriah Smith entered Phillips Academy in Exeter, New Hampshire, where he studied to become a teacher. Already an accomplished writer and artist, he was also class poet at the academy. *Photo provided by Phillips Academy, Exeter, New Hampshire.*

Above: The West Wilton, New Hampshire, birthplace and childhood home of Annie and Uriah Smith. *Photo by Carolyn Weir.*
Below: Saratoga Springs, New York, c. 1890. James White's printing business was based here for a short time in 1851 and 1852. *Photo provided by the Historical Society of Saratoga Springs, New York.*

This painting is believed to be a self-portrait of Annie Smith, older sister to Uriah. Annie served as assistant to *Review and Herald* editor James White and authored several hymns, including "The Blessed Hope." During James White's frequent travels, Annie actually functioned as the *Review* editor, technically making her the first woman to hold the post.
Photo provided by the Ellen G. White Estate.

Joseph Bates, during which she came to see the importance of the seventh-day Sabbath and the urgency of the three angels' messages. She was so convinced that she left her studies and moved to Saratoga Springs, New York, to work with James White in the small publishing business recently set up there. For a time Uriah joined her, working as an engraver on several publications, though he could not sympathize with her beliefs. But in 1852, in the Washington meetinghouse, that began to change. Here's what he says of that time:

Partial text visible within and around the illustration:

cepts of God's law, which pointed out their duty to God; the other contained the last six precepts, pointing out their duty to each other. Then the law of God may be fitly represented by a tree with two large branches, and from these two,

en small branches. One large branch represents love to God, the other, love to one another, [see Deut. vi, 5; Lev. xix, 18,] and the ten branches growing out of the two, represent the several articles of God's law as they are given in Ex.

Above: An illustration by Uriah Smith in the *Advent Review and Sabbath Herald* of March 23, 1852, presenting the relationship between the Ten Commandments and Christ's two laws, "Love God with all thy heart" and "Love thy neighbor as thyself." The engraving was completed before Uriah was convinced of the sanctity of the Sabbath.
Photo provided by the Review and Herald Publishing Association.

"I was in the message of 1843-44, and have ever believed that they meant something. In all the scattering and dividing which followed the passing of that time, I gave little attention to the subject till after the Washington, New Hampshire, conference last fall. Since then an examination of the arguments of our position has fully decided me to go with the remnant, who keep the commandments of God, and the faith of Jesus." [14]

Uriah Smith joined the infant organization full-time in 1853 and served as the editor of the *Advent Review and Sabbath Herald* for more than 40 years.

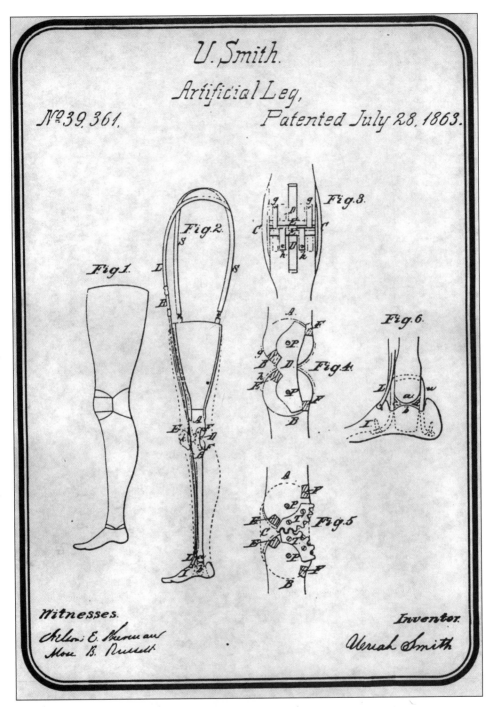

An accomplished inventor, Uriah Smith patented and sold the design for a flexible wooden leg he had initially made for himself. He also invented a school desk with a unique folding seat, and set up a small company to manufacture them. With the profits from these ventures he was able to build himself a new house in Battle Creek, Michigan.
Photo provided by the Loma Linda University Heritage Room.

Cynthia Farnsworth, daughter of John Stowell and second wife of William. They were married September 19, 1855. *Photo provided by the Ellen G. White Estate.*

The Washington congregation was composed of independent, sometimes headstrong, individuals and contentions often arose. Worcester Ball was often in the middle of them. One day he confronted a woman in the congregation about her dress, which he considered to be immodest. Harold Farnsworth describes the confrontation:

> "Hosea Dodge spoke up and said, 'Worcester, have you never read where it says, "Thou shalt not rebuke the daughter of my people"? The next week Worcester came to Brother Dodge and said that during the past week he had gone all through his Bible but had not been able to find the text. . . . Hosea got a twinkle in his eye as he replied, 'Worcester, I didn't say it was in the Bible; I just asked you, "Have you never read?"'" [15]

Alton Farnsworth, right, the eighteenth child of William, and his younger brother Ernest, number 21, about 1936. *Photo provided by the Ellen G. White Estate.*

Above: Getting to the church on time had a different meaning in the 1880s. On horseback, or in open carriages and wagons, members needed a strong commitment to attend when the weather was less favorable than depicted here by artist Vernon Nye.

Left: During the 1800s it was common for members to purchase the pews on which they sat, as a means of providing the funds to construct the building. Because of this, individuals became identified with specific locations in the room. William Farnsworth, it is believed, took his seat to the speaker's right, in the rows beneath the small banner. *Photos provided by the Review and Herald Publishing Association.*

After one church squabble Daniel Farnsworth was heard to say, "A little less 'straight testimony' and a little more straight living will be better for all of us." [16]

James White was constrained to plead, "Brethren in New Hampshire, get humble, and pray in faith to the living God to meet us in power in Washington. Have you little trials? Settle them at once, leave them at home, or stay at home yourself. It is too late to have the work of God hindered by petty trials." [17]

Rochester, New York, where James and Ellen White set up the infant publishing work in 1852. The small group endured great privation in those early years. Potatoes were too expensive, so the group ate porridge, turnips, and beans. After a few weeks, the newly arrived Uriah Smith remarked, "I don't mind eating beans for 365 days in succession, but if they should become a regular diet, I must protest." *Illustration provided by the Review and Herald Publishing Association.*

By 1852 the work of the *Advent Review and Sabbath Herald,* having recently moved to Rochester, had grown into a thriving operation. James White rented a large house on Mount Hope Avenue, where the staff and their families lived and worked. A brand-new hand press was installed in their sitting room. Ellen White described the scene:

"You would smile could you look in upon us and see our furniture. We have bought two old bedsteads for twenty-five cents each. My husband brought me home six old chairs, no two of them alike, for which he paid one dollar. . . . Our first meals were taken on a fireboard placed upon two empty flour barrels." [18]

The work was expanding, and the house was soon filled. James and Ellen White, now with their infant son, Edson; Stephen and Sarah Belden; John Andrews; and Annie Smith—all in their 20s. Annie's brother, Uriah, who joined them later, was 20. Lumen Masten, 23, ran the press. And 13-year-old Warren Bacheller helped him. [19]

J. Warren Bacheller and Homer H. Aldrich were the two principal printers employed by the Review and Herald in 1868. Bacheller first began working in James White's printshop in Rochester at age 13. *Photo provided by the Review and Herald Publishing Association.*

Ellen White, far left, with Willie, James, and Edson in 1864. Their oldest son, Henry, had died only the year before at age 16. *Photo provided by the Ellen G. White Estate.*

Annie Smith contracted tuberculosis while living in Rochester, most likely in the close quarters she shared with James White's infected brother, Nathaniel, and sister, Anna. She went home to West Wilton, New Hampshire, where she died on July 26, 1855. She was just 27 years old. *Photo provided by the Review and Herald Publishing Association.*

In December 1852 James White's brother Nathaniel and sister Anna joined the group. Both were suffering from tuberculosis. Within six months Nathaniel White was dead of the disease. A year later, so was Lumen Masten. In November 1854 Anna White died. And Annie Smith went home to West Wilton, also stricken with tuberculosis. Joseph Bates came to visit her in February of 1855. Annie's mother, Rebekah Smith, says of this visit:

> "At the commencement of the Sabbath . . . the spirit and power of God descended upon her, and she praised God with a loud voice. Brother Bates then said to Annie, 'You needed this blessing, and now if the Lord sees that it is best for you to be laid away in the grave, He will go with you.' "[20]

Tuberculosis was nineteenth-century America's number one killer. Forty-four-year-old naturalist Henry David Thoreau succumbed to "consumption," as it was known, in 1862. *Photo provided by the University of Washington.*

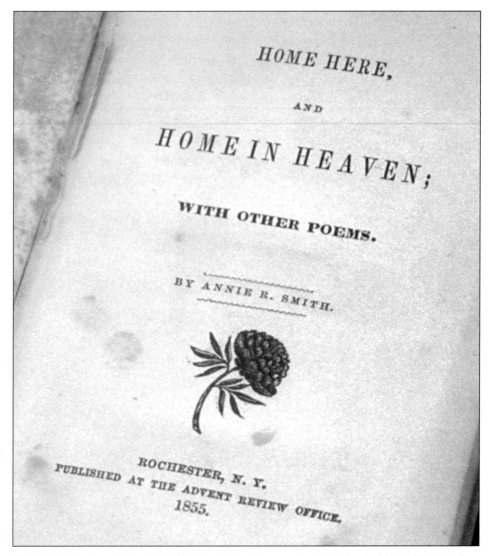

HOME HERE,

AND

HOME IN HEAVEN;

WITH OTHER POEMS.

BY ANNIE R. SMITH.

ROCHESTER, N. Y.
PUBLISHED AT THE ADVENT REVIEW OFFICE.
1855.

Shortly before her death, Annie Smith collected her poems into a book, *Home Here, and Home in Heaven*. Her brother Uriah engraved a woodcut of her favorite flower, the peony, for the title page. The book was published in 1855, after Annie's death. *Photo provided by the Ellen G. White Estate.*

Uriah returned home in May in time to help Annie prepare a book of poems for publication. He sketched and engraved an illustration of her favorite flower, a peony, for the title page. The book was finished in mid-July; Annie Smith died less than 10 days later.[21] Her book of poems, including the poem "Home Here and Home in Heaven," was published by James White in Rochester in 1855.

The number of Sabbathkeepers in Washington continued to grow, until by the mid-1850s they outnumbered their former Christian Brethren, and the meetinghouse came into the possession of the Sabbathkeepers once again. There is no record of any formal transfer. It's likely that as the one congregation increased, the other decreased, and as a number of Sabbathkeepers had been prominent in the company that built the church, they naturally took possession.[22]

Interior view of the Washington meeting-house. *Photo by Elizabeth Howe.*

Aerial view of the Washington Town Center. *Photo provided by the Washington town office.*

About this time Frederick Wheeler began to reach out to other communities. In 1852 he was visiting and holding meetings in the towns of Bennington, Bradford, and Warner, New Hampshire, and over the border in West Hartford, Vermont. In early 1853 he was near Gorham, Maine, when Ellen White's brother Robert died from tuberculosis. Wheeler presented the funeral sermon.[23] Henrietta Kolb remembers Wheeler's ministry:

"I can still remember eagerly watching to see him come in sight, sitting up straight in his open buggy, drawn by Billy, his faithful old gray horse. We saw no ministers in those early days except on these occasions, and what a treat it was![24]

Robert Harmon, Jr., Ellen White's elder brother, died of tuberculosis on February 5, 1853, at age 26. *Photo provided by the Ellen G. White Estate.*

Originally a Methodist preacher, Wheeler became convinced of the Advent message and soon the Sabbath, adopting it in the spring of 1844. On March 16, while residing in Hillsborough, New Hampshire, he preached what is believed to be the first Adventist sermon in favor of the seventh-day Sabbath. He died in 1910, at age 99. *Photo provided by the Ellen G. White Estate.*

The next year Frederick Wheeler ranged even farther, holding meetings in Maine, Vermont, and Massachusetts. His enthusiasm and energy impressed James White, who urged him to move to a more favorable location for his work. At first Wheeler refused, feeling his obligations in Washington and to his congregation there prevented it. But in February 1857, while he was attending a conference in Roosevelt, New York, the way opened:

> "It was decided that the labors of Brother F. Wheeler of New Hampshire are needed in central New York, and that it is the duty of the church to defray the expenses of removing his family to his field of labor, and support him in the field."[25]

It was perhaps the first instance of the still-forming Sabbathkeeping Adventist organization calling a preacher from one field of labor to another, and paying his moving expenses. For several years Wheeler worked with S. W. Rhodes and, later, Hiram Edson, conducting evangelistic services, most often inside a portable tent designed for the purpose. He eventually settled on a farm in West Monroe, New York. Looking back on his life, he wrote:

Hiram Edson

> "I praise God that I have ever been permitted, not only to believe the truth, but to labor somewhat in connection with the work, and that through God's blessing on my feeble efforts some have been led to rejoice in the light and in hope of eternal life through Him." [26]

Frederick Wheeler died on October 11, 1910. He was 99 years old.

Millpond outside a sawmill near Hillsborough, New Hampshire. *Photo provided by Phelps Photo.*

Ellen White about 1864. *Photo provided by the Ellen G. White Estate.*

Above: While living on Wood Street, Ellen White wrote *Spiritual Gifts*, volume 1, the first edition of what is now known as *The Great Controversy*.
Left: In Battle Creek, Michigan, James White built this small home on Wood Street in 1856. *Photos provided by the Ellen G. White Estate.*

Sometime in 1857 Ellen White wrote a letter to Stephen Smith, who was then living in Unity, New Hampshire, perhaps an hour's ride from Washington. When it arrived, Smith feared it was a testimony sent to correct him, and he refused to open it. But as he couldn't bring himself to throw it away, he locked it in a large trunk and soon forgot about it.[27]

In 1855 James White moved from Rochester, New York, to a new two-story wooden structure on West Main and Washington streets in Battle Creek, Michigan. The building was moved in 1861, and in its place this two-story brick building 26' x 66' (8 m. x 20 m.) was erected. The publishing house expanded rapidly, and by the 1890s subsequent additions brought the main building to enclose a total area of 80,000 square feet (7,400 square meters). *All photos on pages 98 and 99 provided by the Review and Herald Publishing Association.*

CHAPTER 7:

Revival

By 1861 the work of the *Advent Review and Sabbath Herald,* now in Battle Creek, Michigan, had expanded to the point that a formal organization was needed. On May 3 the Seventh-day Adventist Publishing Association was established. Eight months later, at the Washington meetinghouse, a two-day organizational meeting was held for the purpose of establishing the first Seventh-day Adventist church in that place.[1] Its charter read as follows:

James White in 1874

"We the undersigned hereby associate our-
selves together as a church, taking the name
Seventh-day Adventists, and covenanting to
keep the commandments of God, and the
faith of Jesus Christ."[2]

Pressmen with their
machines in the new
publishing house

Meeting for Organization.

The Sabbath keepers in Washington N.H.
met for Organization Jan, 12: 1862. when the
following business was transacted
1st. Chose Eld. A Stone Chairman.
2nd. Chose Joshua Philbrick Sec,
3d. Voted to receive the following persons into
Church fellowship viz. Wm Farnsworth,
Newell Mead, Emily Richardson. Martha E.
Philbrick, Lucy A. Dodge. Leonora Smith.
Sarah Mead. Cyrus K. Farnsworth. Harriet
Farnsworth. Joshua Philbrick. Alden Green.
4th. Voted to adopt the Church Covenant as set
forth in the Battle Creek Conference.
5th. Voted to adjourn untill 9. Oclock A.M. Jan 13.
    Met Jan 13th. According to appointment.
1st. Voted to receive into Church fellowship, Cyrus.
Colby. Howard P. Wakefield. Aseneth Wakefield.
Emma Wakefield.
2nd. Voted to abstain from the use of Tobacco Tea, Coffee,
wearing of Hoops, or Jewelry.

The Washington, New Hampshire, congregation of Sabbathkeepers officially became Seventh-day Adventists in January 1862, "covenanting to keep the commandments of God, and the faith of Jesus Christ." *Photo provided by the Ellen G. White Estate.*

Washington is credited with being the birthplace of the Seventh-day Adventist Church. *Photo by Elizabeth Howe.*

Eleven persons were received into church fellowship that Saturday night, and four more Sunday morning, making a total of 15.[3] Along with accepting the name, they also voted to abstain from the use of tobacco, tea, coffee, wearing of hoops, and jewelry. In 1863 a Sabbath school was formed for the children in the community. One hardy soul who was present at this meeting wrote:

> "Notwithstanding the bad roads, we had a good gathering. . . . We felt as though Jesus and [His] holy angels smiled upon His people which were trying to benefit the young."[4]

According to the records kept in New Haven, Connecticut, the winter of 1867 ranked as the fourth coldest in New England's history. A major snowstorm in mid-December dumped 12 inches (30 centimeters) of snow in New York City and piled up drifts three feet (.9 meters) deep, closing down train yards as far north as Portland, Maine. For 35 consecutive days the mercury stood at zero or below in Concord, New Hampshire, a record at the time. That winter, snowfall there totaled 69 inches (1.75 meters). *Photo provided by Phelps Photo.*

The Washington, New Hampshire, church has fallen into disrepair from time to time over the years, yet a Seventh-day Adventist congregation has met there continually since the church was incorporated in 1862. *Photo provided by the Review and Herald Publishing Association.*

It was a promising beginning, but it didn't last. Without the guiding hand of Frederick Wheeler the congregation developed problems. Criticism set in. Worcester Ball openly opposed the work of Ellen White and began writing articles attacking her.[5] Younger members, such as Eugene Farnsworth, the ninth child of William, were influenced by these criticisms and lost interest in the church. By 1867 the congregation had dwindled to the point that they were no longer even holding services.[6]

William Farnsworth, who had struggled for years to quit chewing tobacco, now fell back into his old habit. As a leader in the church, he tried to keep it secret, but it wasn't an easy habit to hide. While working in the forest one winter day, Eugene saw his father kicking fresh snow over the stains he left behind.

Eugene Farnsworth considered a career in law, yet a chance meeting with J. N. Andrews while weeding a vegetable patch, turned him onto the ministry. *Photo provided by the Review and Herald Publishing Association.*

Above: Until the early twentieth century, wood was an essential fuel in winter or summer, and collecting it was a constant task. Summer kitchens were often built to keep the heat generated by cooking stoves out of the house. *Engraving provided by the Library of Congress.* **Below:** One of the many unpaved lanes found throughout the Washington area. *Photo provided by Phelps Photo.*

Right: Battle Creek's most famous citizen was ex-slave, abolitionist, temperance advocate, and pioneer for womens' rights Sojourner Truth, who resided there for 26 years. Truth occasionally spoke at Adventist gatherings, though she is not thought to have been a part of the Millerite movement in the 1840s. *Photo provided by the Sojourner Truth Institute of Battle Creek.*

Below: John Nevins Andrews once considered a career in law, hoping to follow in the footsteps of his uncle Charles, a congressman, who offered to pay his way through law school. However, early in 1845, at age 15, John accepted the Sabbath from a tract written by T. M. Preble. It changed the direction of his life. *Photo provided by the Ellen G. White Estate.*

In Battle Creek, Michigan, in May 1867, John Nevins Andrews was elected the third president of the General Conference of Seventh-day Adventists, following the term of James White.[7] Andrews spent much of his time that year visiting the established churches in New England. During the summer he came to Washington.[8] He was discouraged by what he saw and heard. Among the members he found criticism, frustration, and apathy. Almost no young people attended the services he conducted in the meetinghouse. When asked about this, one teenager replied, "They're all hypocrites in there."[9]

In November James and Ellen White determined to return to Washington, probably at Andrews' urging, and in December they traveled there in hopes of sparking a revival. Andrews sent out an invitation:

> "We expect that these will be large gatherings of the friends of the cause, especially of the old friends of Brother and Sister White. . . . Come with your provisions, your blankets, quilts, comfortables, buffalo robes, and your straw ticks to be filled at the place of meeting."[10]

Moonlight Sleighride, by W. Wellstood, 1886. The Whites would have ridden in a sleigh much like this one to Washington, New Hampshire, from Battle Creek, Michigan, in December 1867. The trip of approximately 800 miles (1,300 kilometers), taken in winter, was a clear sign of the concern James and Ellen White felt for the Washington members. *Illustration provided by the Library of Congress.*

The first meeting began at 10:00 a.m. on Monday, December 23, and lasted for six hours.[11] Even though the weather had turned very cold and it had been snowing heavily for several days, the people came anyway.[12] Everyone knew of the special ministry of Ellen White, and some, like young Eugene Farnsworth, had doubts about the authority of her inspired counsels. Yet whatever their expectations, God did not disappoint them.

Rising to her feet, Mrs. White looked around at her audience. One by one she singled out individuals in the congregation. She spoke to them directly, revealing details about their lives that were not publicly known. "I have been shown," she said. She praised those who were facing personal trials and rebuked those who were causing them. Again and again she identified cheats, backsliders, and saints alike.

The Washington meetinghouse has often been filled to capacity, as it was in August 1944 during a celebration marking 100 years of Sabbathkeeping Adventism. Here, Elder A. Ruf presides over a shoulder-to-shoulder Sabbath school class. *Photo provided by the Review and Herald Publishing Association.*

E. G. White with her eldest sister, Caroline Clough, July 1872. *Photo provided by the Ellen G. White Estate.*

Eugene Farnsworth was impressed. Ellen White's accuracy was remarkable, he thought, but not entirely convincing. Many of the details she revealed he could have told her about himself, and maybe someone had. If she is really inspired of God, he thought, she would tackle the case of my father. At almost that moment Ellen White turned her attention to William Farnsworth.

> "Brother Farnsworth, I have been shown you have a problem with tobacco. But the worst of the matter is that you are acting the part of the hypocrite, trying to deceive your brethren into thinking you have discarded it, as you promised to do when you united with the church."[13]

William Farnsworth

When Ellen White finished speaking, the members rose, one by one, including William Farnsworth, to acknowledge the accuracy of her observations. That was enough for Eugene—and for many others. A spirit of repentance and confession filled the room,

The Cyrus Farnsworth home after a heavy snow. Millen Pond lies just out of frame beyond the lower right corner. It is a long-held tradition that this was the site where the icy baptisms took place, with the warmth of the Farnsworth home only a short distance away.
Photo provided by Ken and Betty Brighton, the current owners.

Ice Cutting, by Francis W. Tolman, a linoleum block print. Ice harvesting was a big business in northern regions, providing ice for refrigeration all year round.
Illustration courtesy of Barry Tolman. Woodcut provided by Richard Schlecht.

and a true reformation was begun. Even Worcester Ball was silenced and for a time became a vigorous advocate of Ellen White and her testimonies.

The young people in the church were moved by the experience of their parents. At a service on Christmas Day, 13 young people stood and requested immediate baptism, Eugene Farnsworth being one of them. Five others joined them later.[14] Faced with the determination of these young people, a hole was cut through two feet of ice on Millen Pond, and 12 of them were baptized.[15]

The church at Washington never again fell into the discouragement and loss it had experienced before 1867.

The Washington church today. *Photo by Joshua Rodman.*

After a long career as conference president, evangelist, and committee member, Eugene Farnsworth died in 1935, at 87 years of age. *Photo provided by the Review and Herald Publishing Association.*

CHAPTER 8:

Surrender

Eugene Farnsworth grew up to become a minister. He worked primarily in the Midwest, serving churches in Iowa, Nebraska, Dakota, and Nevada. In 1877 he became the president of the Iowa-Nebraska Conference of Seventh-day Adventists, though he spent most of his time in active evangelism.

In the summer of 1885 Eugene determined to visit his father, William, who was now almost 80. He arranged to return home for a short visit and was invited to preach on the three Sabbaths he would be at the Washington meetinghouse.[1]

The Seventh-day Adventist Church grew rapidly after 1868, with membership reaching more than 20,000 by 1885. Here, members enjoy a noontime meal at a camp meeting in Minnesota in 1875. *Photo provided by the Review and Herald Publishing Association.*

Matilda Smith kept her connection to the church through the years that her husband, Stephen, turned his back on it. Because of her faithfulness, he repented and his influence for good has far exceeded what harm he might have provoked in his earlier years *Photo provided b the Ellen G. White Estate.*

As Eugene mounted the pulpit to speak, he noticed a familiar face in the congregation—Stephen Smith. An old man now, Smith had not worshiped in that church for more than 25 years, and at first Eugene was uncertain what he might do. But Stephen Smith had changed.

Matilda Smith never shared her husband's disillusionment with the Adventist leaders in Battle Creek. Ignoring Stephen's protests, she maintained a subscription to the *Advent Review and Sabbath Herald* and, with it, her connection to the church. One day in 1884 Stephen Smith happened upon a copy of the *Review.* An article by Ellen White was prominently featured, and he began to read. He was surprised to discover he agreed with it. The next week he found another article by her, and he agreed with it as well.

As he continued to read, from week to week, he came to realize how wrong he had been. Remembering the letter Ellen White had written to him all those years before, he went back to the trunk and found it where he had hidden it. For the first time, he read the letter.

For many years Ellen White wrote a devotional article for almost every issue of the *Advent Review and Sabbath Herald*. This article from the March 4, 1884, issue was adapted from a sermon she gave during the 1883 General Conference session. Its topic would have found particular resonance with Stephen Smith. *Photo provided by the Review and Herald Publishing Association.*

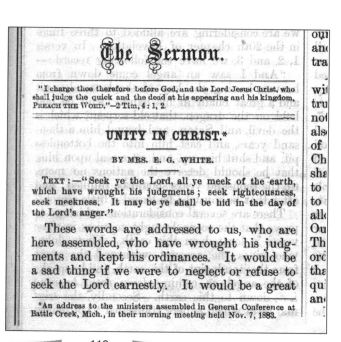

The Sermon.

"I charge thee therefore before God, and the Lord Jesus Christ, who shall judge the quick and the dead at his appearing and his kingdom, PREACH THE WORD."—2 Tim. 4 : 1, 2.

UNITY IN CHRIST.*

BY MRS. E. G. WHITE.

TEXT : —"Seek ye the Lord, all ye meek of the earth, which have wrought his judgments ; seek righteousness, seek meekness. It may be ye shall be hid in the day of the Lord's anger."

These words are addressed to us, who are here assembled, who have wrought his judgments and kept his ordinances. It would be a sad thing if we were to neglect or refuse to seek the Lord earnestly. It would be a great

*An address to the ministers assembled in General Conference at Battle Creek, Mich., in their morning meeting held Nov. 7, 1883.

Many of the leading figures in the Washington, New Hampshire, story are buried in the little cemetery that adjoins the churchyard. *Photo provided by the Review and Herald Publishing Association.*

Her words presented an accurate description of Stephen Smith's life—the bitterness and disappointment, the loss and the pain, that would be his if he refused to change his course. And everything had happened just as she had said. Ellen White had clearly seen where his stubbornness would lead and tried to warn him. But he had ignored her, and her warnings had come true.

Eugene Farnsworth in 1926. *Photo provided by the Ellen G. White Estate.*

Stephen Smith faithfully attended the services in the meetinghouse, listening intently and without objection, as Eugene Farnsworth presented biblical support for the gift of prophecy and the special ministry of Ellen White. When Eugene had finished speaking, Smith rose to his feet. Everyone who knew him wondered what he might say. But it was their turn to be surprised.

Above: The Battle Creek Sanitarium brought the Adventist health message worldwide attention.

Right: This 1879 photograph is the last taken of James White before his death. Years of overwork and stress plagued him with ill health, so in 1879 he and Ellen avoided the harsh Michigan winter by moving to Texas for a time. But they were back in Battle Creek when James White died on August 6, 1881, of a sudden illness, just two days after his sixtieth birthday. *Photos provided by the Ellen G. White Estate.*

Below: The first Adventist camp meeting in Europe was held in early June 1887, among the pines of Bellevue Grove on Jel Island in Moss, Norway. Ellen White is seated to the right of the tent, with her son W. C. White standing behind her. Ellen was nearing the end of a two-year stay spent traveling throughout Europe, counseling the missions there, planning the Conflict of the Ages series, and visiting in person places she'd seen in vision. *Photo provided by the Ellen G. White Estate.*

[111]

CENTRAL S. D. A. PUBLISHING HOUSE,
BATTLE CREEK, MICH.

The Review and Herald Publishing Association in Battle Creek, Michigan, had grown into a substantial business by the late 1800s. But many were troubled by the practices its success fostered. In a letter to the Review board in November 1901 Ellen White wrote, "I have been almost afraid to open the *Review,* fearing to see that God has cleansed the publishing house by fire."—*Testimonies,* vol. 8, p. 91. A little more than a year later the building burned to the ground. *Photo provided by the Review and Herald Publishing Association.*

"I don't want you to be afraid of me, brethren, for I haven't come to criticize you—I've quit that kind of business. No honest man can help seeing that God is with the Advent movement. . . . I want to be in fellowship with this people in heart and in the church.

"I have come to that place where I finally believe the testimonies are all of God. . . . I thought I knew as much as an 'old woman's visions,' as I used to term them. May God forgive me. But to my sorrow I found the visions were right, and the man who thought he knew it all was all wrong. . . .

The only known photograph of Stephen Smith, taken around 1880. *Photo provided by the Ellen G. White Estate.*

"Brethren, I'm too old to undo what I've done. I'm too feeble to get out to our large meetings, but I want you to tell our people everywhere that another rebel has surrendered."[2]

Two visitors to the Washington, New Hampshire, meetinghouse sometime in the 1920s, judging by their clothing. *Photo by T. M. French.*

Ripples

The Seventh-day Adventist Church has grown until, at the beginning the new millennium, it includes millions of members in more than 200 countries around the world. But it all began in this simple frame building in New Hampshire, where, in response to God's leading, a small group of people stepped out in faith to keep all 10 of God's commandments, including the fourth, which designates the seventh day of the week as His holy day. Like ripples from a pebble dropped in a pond of water, the truth embraced at Washington, New Hampshire, continues to spread throughout the entire world.

An outdoor meeting held in Mwanza, Tanzania, in July 2001. *Photo by Benny Moore.*

Above: Grave marker for Worcester Ball in the Washington Church Cemetery.

Right: Ellen White's grandson, Elder Arthur White, stood next to a tower of her published work—some 70 books in all—stacked on the floor of the White Estate vault in Washington, D.C., about 1960. Ellen White's active leadership of the Seventh-day Adventist Church spanned more than 60 years. *Photo provided by the Ellen G. White Estate.*

Right: Joseph Bates wrote up his life story, with its tales of kidnapping, pirates, and temperance, and anti-slavery advocacy, for the Adventist publication *Youth's Instructor.* The narrative was released in book form under the title *Autobiography* in 1868. He eventually settled in Monterey, Michigan, where he continued to be a strong advocate of health reform and the seventh-day Sabbath. He was often heard to exclaim on his way to church, "Oh! How I love this Sabbath!" He died in 1872 at the age of 79. *Photo provided by the Review and Herald Publishing Association.*

Cyrus Farnsworth often felt the misfortunes of life. In 1847 he married Delight Oaks, the young schoolteacher to whom he had rented a room in his house. But she died unexpectedly in August 1858, leaving him with three boys—the youngest barely 4 years old. He married Lydia Knight just two months later, but she also died suddenly in the spring of 1861. That autumn he married yet again, this time to Harriet Camp, a wife who—perhaps much to his relief—finally outlived him. He died on April 6, 1899, and she 22 years later. This photograph shows the sunburned Cyrus with Harriet and their teenage daughter Ida, about 1880. *Photo provided by the Review and Herald Publishing Association.*

Left: Many of Washington's faithful believers, Cyrus Farnsworth among them, await the resurrection morning only a few dozen feet from the small meetinghouse where they made the most important decisions of their lives. *Photo by Elizabeth Howe.*

The Town Center, Washington, New Hampshire. *Photo by Elizabeth Howe.*

References

Chapter 1: Liberal Principles

[1] *History of Washington, New Hampshire, 1768-1886* (Washington, N.H.: Washington History Committee, 1976), p 19.

[2] *Ibid.,* p. 397.

[3] *Ibid.,* p. 16.

[4] Ronald Jager and Grace Jager, *Portrait of a Hill Town: A History of Washington, New Hampshire, 1876-1976* (Warner, N.H.: R. C. Brayshaw and Co., 1998), p. 534.

[5] Bert Haloviak, "Some Great Connexions: Our Seventh-day Adventist Heritage From the Christian Church" (unpublished manuscript, General Conference of SDA, 1994), p 1.

[6] *Ibid.,* p. 4.

[7] *History of Washington, New Hampshire, 1768-1886,* p. 269.

[8] Letter from Natalie B. Perkins, Deputy Register, Sullivan County, New Hampshire, Registry of Deeds, to Julia Neuffer, Dec. 30, 1969.

[9] Christian Brethren, "Constitution Upon Which the Meeting House Is to Be Built," in Jager and Jager, p. 534.

Mark Ford prepares to photograph the hand-hewn rafters of the Washington meeting-house. *Photo by Elizabeth Howe.*

Washington selectman Rufford Harrison (left) talks with author Mark Ford atop the Washington Town Center's bell tower during production of the companion video to this book, also called *The Church at Washington, New Hampshire.* Besides being an able local historian, Mr. Harrison is a talented character actor and portrays the voice of Archibald White, who in 1776 petitioned the General Assembly of New Hampshire to change the name of the town from Camden to Washington. Mr. White was successful, as was Mr. Harrison. *Photo by Charles Smith.*

[10] George Wheeler, interview at West Monroe, New York, with C. E. Eldridge and Bessie J. Rice, May 5, 1934.

[11] *Record Book of the First Christian Society in Washington, New Hampshire,* p. 4. In D. E. Robinson, "Early Sabbathkeeping in Washington, New Hampshire, and Vicinity" (unpublished manuscript, General Conference of SDA, 1940), p. 1.

[12] C. L. Taylor, "As the Days of a Tree," *Review and Herald,* Aug. 30, 1956.

Chapter 2: Millerites

[1] Don F. Neufeld and Julia Neuffer, eds., *Seventh-day Adventist Bible Students' Source Book* (Washington, D.C.: Review and Herald Pub. Assn., 1962), pp. 313-315.

[2] Denison Olmsted, "Observations on the Meteors of November 13th, 1833," *American Journal of Science and Arts 25* ([January] 1834): 363. In *SDA Bible Students' Source Book,* p. 409.

[3] Frederick Douglass, *Life and Times of Frederick Douglass* (New York: Pathway Press, 1941), p. 117. In *SDA Bible Students' Source Book,* p. 413.

[4] William Miller, *William Miller's Apology and Defense* (Borton: J. V. Himes, 1845), pp. 12, 13.

[5] Godfrey T. Anderson, *Outrider of the Apocalypse: Life and Times of Joseph Bates* (Mountain View, Calif.: Pacific Press Pub. Assn., 1972), p. 46.

[6] Ronald L. Numbers and Jonathan M. Butler, eds., *The Disappointed* (Indianapolis: Indiana University Press, 1987), p. 30.

[7] *Ibid.,* p. 82.

[8] *Ibid.,* p. 46.

[9] Haloviak, p. 2.

[10] Anderson, p. 50.

[11] H. A. Larrabee, "Trumpeter of Doomsday," *American Heritage,* April 1964. In Anderson, p. 45.

[12] See Isaac C. Wellcome, *History of the Second Advent Message* (Yarmouth, Maine: I. E. Wellcome, 1874), p. 206.

[13] Taylor.

[14] Haloviak, p. 2.

[15] Taylor.

[16] Haloviak, p. 13.

Graffiti left behind by a bored young scholar at the Penniman school. *Photo by Elizabeth Howe.*

Ron Jager, together with his wife, Grace, literally wrote the book on Washington, New Hampshire. Their 1977 history *Portrait of a Hill Town*, as well as their other works on New England, provided many new facts that helped tie the Adventist story together. Jager was also the narrator for the companion video to this work, *The Church at Washington, New Hampshire*.
Photo by Mark Ford.

[17] James and Ellen White, *Life Sketches* (Battle Creek, Mich: Seventh-day Adventist Pub. Assn., 1880), pp. 125, 126.

Chapter 3: Sabbathkeepers

[1] Merlin D Burt, "Rachel Oaks Preston, A Review of Her Life and Experience" (unpublished manuscript, General Conference of SDA, 1996), p. 3.

[2] *Ibid.*

[3] *Ibid.*

[4] D. E. Robinson, "Sabbathkeeping in Washington, New Hampshire," (unpublished manuscript, General Conference of SDA, 1935), p. 2.

[5] F. W. Bartle to William A. Spicer. In William A. Spicer, *Pioneer Days* (Washington, D.C.: Review and Herald Pub. Assn., 1941), pp. 122, 123.

[6] Taylor.

[7] Don F. Neufeld, ed., *Seventh-day Adventist Encyclopedia* (Hagerstown, Md.: Review and Herald Pub. Assn., 1996), vol. 11, pp. 77, 78.

[8] In Numbers and Butler, p. 29.

[9] *Seventh-day Adventist Encyclopedia,* vol. 11, p. 620.

[10] James White, *Life Incidents* (Battle Creek, Mich: Seventh-day Adventist Pub. Assn., 1868), p. 166.

[11] In Numbers and Butler, p. 219.

[12] John N. Loughborough, *The Great Second Advent Movement*

Mark Harris

Phil Barker

(Washington, D.C.: Review and Herald Pub. Assn., 1905), p. 116.

[13] George Wheeler interview.

[14] In Numbers and Butler, p. 209.

[15] George Knight, *Millennial Fever* (Boise, Idaho: Pacific Press Pub. Assn., 1993), p. 214.

[16] In Numbers and Butler, p. 53.

[17] In James White, *Life Incidents,* pp. 177, 178.

Chapter 4: The Disappointment

[1] In John Orr Corliss, "The Message and Its Friends—No 2, Joseph Bates as I Knew Him," *Review and Herald,* Aug. 16, 1923.

[2] In Numbers and Butler, p. 215.

[3] William Miller to I. O. Orr, M.D., Dec. 13, 1844.

[4] In Numbers and Butler, pp. 222, 223.

[5] Francis D Nichol, *The Midnight Cry* (Washington, D.C.: Review and Herald Pub. Assn., 1944), pp. 274, 275.

[6] George Wheeler interview.

[7] William Miller to Joshua V. Himes, Nov. 10, 1844. In *The Midnight Cry,* Dec. 5, 1844, p. 180.

[8] Sylvester Bliss, *The Memoirs of William Miller* (Boston: Joshua V. Himes, 1853), p. 378.

Elizabeth Howe was the principal researcher and photo archivist for this book and its companion video documentary. *Photo by Rob Pohle.*

Chapter 5: What's the News?

[1] *SDA Encyclopedia,* vol. 10, p. 541.

[2] Mabel Robinson Miller, *William and His 22* (Washington, D.C.: Review and Herald Pub. Assn., 1959), pp. 14, 157, 158.

[3] *Ibid.,* p. 54.

[4] James Nix, unpublished communication.

[5] S. N. Haskell in *General Conference Bulletin* 1909, p. 290.

[6] Arthur Whitefield Spalding, *Origin and History of Seventh-day Adventists* (Washington, D.C.: Review and Herald Pub. Assn., 1961), vol. 1, p. 116; Mabel Robinson Miller, p. 68.

[7] *In the Footsteps of the Pioneers* (Silver Spring, Md.: Ellen G. White Estate, General Conference of SDA, 1990), p. 87.

[8] D. E. Robinson, "Early Sabbathkeeping," p. 4.

[9] *Ibid.*

[10] *SDA Encyclopedia,* vol. 1, p. 132.

[11] Haloviak, p. 11.

[12] William A Spicer, *Pioneer Days of the Advent Movement* (Washington, D.C.: Review and Herald Pub. Assn., 1941), p. 48.

[13] In Spicer, p. 49.

[14] George Wheeler interview.

[15] Spalding, vol. 1, p. 121.

[16] *Ibid.*

[17] *In the Footsteps of the Pioneers,* p. 35.

[18] *Seventh-day Adventist Encyclopedia,* vol. 10, p. 171; Ellen G. White, *Life Sketches of Ellen G. White* (Mountain View, Calif.: Pacific Press Pub. Assn., 1915), pp. 100, 101.

[19] *History of Washington, New Hampshire,* 1768-1886, p. 400.

[20] Burt, pp. 4, 5.

[21] Spalding, vol. 1, p. 118.

A rusted basin and some loose foundation stones are all that remain of Simeon Farnsworth's original homestead on Safford's Hill, a short distance from the Town Center. *Photo by Elizabeth Howe.*

Chapter 6: New Directions

[1] Anderson, p. 63.

[2] *Seventh-day Adventist Encyclopedia,* vol. 11, p. 773.

[3] Robert G. Wearner, "The Sabbathkeepers of Washington, New Hampshire" (unpublished manuscript, General Conference of SDA, 1961) p. 1.

Ice cutting

[15] Mabel Robinson Miller, pp. 100–102.

Chapter 8: Surrender

[1] A. L. White, "Stephen Smith and the Unread Testimony," p. 352.

[2] *Ibid.*, pp. 352–354.

Generations of Adventists from all over the world have collected on the steps of the Washington meetinghouse to have their picture taken, perhaps in an effort to identify with the pioneers, to stand where they stood, see what they saw, and perhaps replay for themselves the courageous decisions that have been made there. *Photo provided by the Review and Herald Publishing Association.*